MUSIC THERAPY:
Death and Grief

BY CHAVA SEKELES

Barcelona PUBLISHERS

Distributed throughout the world by:

Barcelona Publishers
4 White Brook Road
Gilsum, N.H. 03448
Tel: 603-357-0236   Fax: 603-357-2073
Web site: www.barcelonapublishers.com
SAN 298-6299

Cover design © 2007 by Frank McShane

Dedicated to

My husband and friend

Eliezer Sekeles

ACKNOWLEDGMENTS

I would like to thank Elizabeth Kay for her meaningful linguistic support and therapeutic wisdom; Professor Kenneth Bruscia for his professionalism, accuracy, and patience; Manfred Hed for his friendship and musicological knowledge; Dr. Jaacov Avni for guiding me in complicated therapeutic situations; and my sons Barak, Raz, and Sharon for their interest and practical support.

Chava Sekeles
Nataf Village, Israel
September 2006

Contents

FOREWORD

This book, as do other works by Dr. Chava Sekeles, exemplifies the special character of the writer and her unique ability not only to address the problems facing her patients, but also to fit to each of them the therapy that will bring maximum success.

In this book, Chava draws from over 40 years of experience, both in Israel and abroad, in the management of patients suffering from the deleterious effects of death and grief. She has managed to eloquently convey her method for the use of music therapy as an effective tool in addressing the special needs of each of the seven patients described in the book, employing a different strategy for each.

The scope of the cases mentioned in the book covers a wide variety of the effects that death and grief have on people of all ages and paints a comprehensive picture of their struggle toward returning to their former love of life. The therapeutic interventions that Chava describes were not always complete or successful, mainly due to the wishes of the patient and/or the family to discontinue treatment, but all manage to create a wealth of knowledge regarding the unique problem of each patient and the strategy Chava employed for each one. The methods used include both receptive and active music therapy, each suited to the special requirements of the patient.

It is impressive to note how much time and effort Chava spent on the initial analysis of each patient, slowly learning his or her specific problem. In each case, the intake covered both physiological and psychological aspects, allowing her to obtain the maximum background for formulating her treatment strategies. The book illuminates her patience and compassion with her patients and her ability to alter the treatment in "real time" so that the patient and his or her family would realize the best possible results from the therapy.

As a layman and nontherapist, I found the chapters describing music as relating to death and grief of special interest. In the chapter on the role of Israeli songs in coping with personal tragedy and the subsequent chapter on the relationship between art music and death and its use in the therapeutic process, Chava has afforded the reader an eloquent, comprehensive, and in-depth insight into these subjects in a manner rarely seen.

The chapter on the effect that the death of a patient has on the music therapist is unique in its contribution to the understanding of the fine line between the close and personal involvement of the therapist during treatment with the patient and his or her immediate surroundings and the position that the therapist takes when a patient passes away. Therapists have a very close and personal relationship with their patients, usually over long periods of time, and their death has a dramatic effect on the therapist. This, of necessity, is a very personal chapter, and describes how Chava has managed to tread that fine line after many years of experience. It also gives guidelines that can be very useful to the development of the therapist (not only the music therapist, but all therapeutic professionals) in how to cope with this very difficult experience.

Chava not only has a wealth of experience, as can easily be seen in this book, but also is able to describe her method and relate the success or failure of the therapeutic process in a lucid and totally engrossing manner. The book is easily understandable by both therapist and layman, but Chava does not compromise on the high professional standards that characterize her. Each chapter is a world unto itself, and each patient develops under the reader's eyes as the narrative goes on.

The methods Chava uses are clearly described for each case, and the relative success of each is carefully and critically analyzed to obtain maximum understanding for future use in similar situations. In addition, the methodology Chava has used can be adapted to fit specific situations that the therapist might encounter in the future. Chava's extensive experience evidenced in this book, as well as her comprehensive use of the relevant literature, enable the reader to learn much from each case. In addition, the understandings brought forth in the more general chapters can be not only an important learning tool for young therapists, but also a unique insight into the world of music therapy for the layman.

Finally, on a personal note, I have known Chava for over 40 years and have cherished every moment of my personal contact with her and her late husband Eliezer. Her fortitude in the face of a series of personal tragedies, her capability to accept and internalize them, and her ability to continue giving of herself to family, friends, and patients has been reciprocated by the trust and love she receives in return. These setbacks have only strengthened her therapeutic capacity, her compassion for her patients, and her resolve toward their return to a normal existence. The dedication of each chapter to a person who has influenced Chava both personally and professionally, and the short biography of each, is an indication of these characteristics.

This book is a testament of the person and professional integrity that exemplify Chava Sekeles. It is a unique and engrossing book, from which I feel I have greatly enriched my knowledge and understanding.

Professor Oren Zinder
Rambam Medical Center and
The Technion Faculty of Medicine
Haifa, Israel
November 2006

INTRODUCTION

During the 44 years in which I have practiced music therapy, I have treated many patients going through the process of mourning, either for a family member, a friend, or for their own medical condition. Over the past 10 years, I have begun collecting and organizing my reports on patients in grief, their musical recordings, theoretical material which deals with the issue, and my own thoughts, in order to construct a solid picture on the subject as elicited during music therapy sessions.

This book consists of 10 chapters, seven of which are case analysis and three that include general subjects I have dealt with during the past 40 years.

The first one, "Life Under Terror: Israeli Songs in Music Therapy," is a case description and analysis concerning *Miri*,[1] a child whose mother and baby brother were killed in a terror attack. Miri suffered from Post Traumatic Stress Disorder, which resulted in, among other things, complete mutism. After some progress, she began to bring to therapy many Israeli songs, which were initially used receptively and later actively.

The second chapter, entitled "The Role of Israeli Songs in Coping With Collective and Personal Grief," deals with the phenomena of Israeli songs and mourning and dwells on the distinct situation facing our country, a country that is in a state of constant war and suffers regularly from terror, traumas, loss, and grief, in which mourning rituals often occur privately as well as nationally. Most people I interviewed on the subject said, "In Israel, one opens the radio and from the music heard can tell that a new catastrophe has occurred."

The third chapter, "The Courage to Die," deals with the therapeutic process undergone by *Nathaniel,* a terminal cancer patient who preferred receptive music therapy, occasionally accompanied by recited poetry. Nathaniel chose to surround himself with beauty, flowers, music, and his family's love. He gradually deteriorated and avoided verbal conversations with even his own wife and children. He died calmly and gracefully.

The fourth chapter, "Where Have All Our Flowers Gone? Music Therapy With a Bereaved Mother and Widow," is the case analysis of *Naama,* whose soldier-son was killed in an army accident during one of the Israeli wars. She later lost her husband, was left with her younger son David, and suffered from a deep depression. Naama's therapy integrated both receptive and active music therapy. She initiated listening to precomposed music either recorded or preferably played live by the therapist, and also agreed to improvise and create her own music. Her therapeutic process concluded with mutual sessions with her son, David.

The fifth chapter is entitled "The Relation Between Art Music,[2] Death, and Grief." Music is the primary tool and language of the music therapist. In order to understand how to use it therapeutically, we should first be acquainted with art music in depth. This is not to say that we should neglect other musical categories, such as ethnic, jazz, popular, traditional, etc. The chapter on art music and death is a general one, which discusses the interrelationship between music and death and the attitude of composers toward the subject. I rarely chose formal music such as the mass requiem, which was intended for bereavement ceremonies, preferring other musical compositions, specifically from the 19th century on.

The sixth chapter, "Bobby Laments His Grandfather," deals with a child at risk who suffered from a developmental disorder and was able to lament his beloved grandfather through music therapy. This very issue had remained suppressed for several years and had placed the burden of unfinished business on young Bobby's shoulders.

The seventh chapter, "To Be Afraid of Your Own Shadow," focuses on *Avi,* a brain-damaged child who suffered from multiple familial losses while living in a settlement behind "the green line." Avi was mainly treated through Sekeles's (1996) Developmental-Integrative Music Therapy,[3] which suited him since he suffered from both neurological dysfunction and psychological traumas.

The eighth chapter, "Mother, the White Dove," describes and analyzes *Jonas,* whose mother died of cancer. Jonas suffered from Borderline Personality Disorder and resisted verbal therapy. Thus, he was sent to music therapy in order to circumvent speech with the hope of developing a different mode of communication.

The ninth chapter is titled and dedicated to "Edwin, Who Murdered His Wife in a Psychotic Attack." Edwin was hospitalized in a psychiatric ward and administered both individual and group music therapy for 5 years. During these years, we often used song writing as the main technique and approach.

Edwin brings us to the 10th and final chapter: "The Grief of the Therapist Over Patients Who Have Passed Away." This subject induced emotional conflict, as it compelled me to open my heart and reveal my personal feelings. Apart from the drive that impelled me to do so, music therapy colleagues encouraged me, arguing that at a certain age and after many years of experience as a therapist, a personal contribution might be of use to the professional public.

While writing the chapters, I was aided by the reports I used to write after each session, the recordings regularly made during the sessions (with the consent of the patients), and theoretical material gathered throughout the world and in Israel (from the fields of psychology, medicine, education, and music therapy). In addition, use was made of results from questionnaires I distributed on different occasions. It is important to mention that administering therapy through a Developmental-Integrative Model enables the therapist to understand and accept each patient as a world in himself, never rigidly adhering to the same theories, practicalities, and techniques. Accordingly, the seven case analyses reflect this variability.

In her book *Supportive Eclectic Music Therapy for Grief and Loss*, Ruth Bright (2002) emphasizes how important it is that therapists who treat patients suffering from death-grief issues acquire a solid philosophy concerning their own attitude toward "death and dying, euthanasia, life after death, chronic disability, old age" (p. 75). Indeed, it would have been difficult to cope with the feelings aroused while administering therapy and to then verbalize and formulate them. I owe the fact that I mustered the courage to do so to my patients, to my colleagues, and to the personal process I underwent with my beloved husband Eliezer. During his terminal illness, we both internalized the concept that death has to be truly and naturally accepted as part of the cycle of life.

Each chapter is dedicated to a person who influenced my personal and professional life. The book as a whole is dedicated to my husband Eliezer.

Notes

(1) All of the names and some details have been changed in order to protect the privacy of the patient and in regulation with the professional ethics of the field.

(2) The Developmental-Integrative Model in Music Therapy (DIMT) is the model that I developed throughout the years and formulated in my 1996 book, *Music: Motion and Emotion*.

(3) "Art music" is a term used in musicology as partly parallel to the popular expression "classical music." The last one has lost its original meaning: 1. A model composition that has survived throughout the centuries. 2. Music that belongs to the 18th century. It is now being used as a general term for music played in concert halls.

MUSIC THERAPY:
Death and Grief

Chapter One

LIFE UNDER TERROR: ISRAELI SONGS IN MUSIC THERAPY

A CASE ANALYSIS

"The day has gone, the night arrived,
the two are taking an eternal slumber,
on the well of blood, on the well of umber"
(from "Ringing Chimes,"[1] lyrics and music by M. Shelem, 1937)

Dedicated to Amos Fink[2]

INTRODUCTION

Miri was 4 years old when referred to music therapy. She was a tiny little girl with curly blond hair and a blank facial expression—save for her searching eyes—with sharp, quick movements, devoid of verbal communication. Miri did not use her voice; neither did she react to the voices of others. She gave me the immediate impression of a little animal, confused in a new cage, using nonstop mobility to survive. I was informed by Miri's father that she could talk, that she was a very intelligent little girl, that her language was extremely advanced, and that her loss of voice was due to a traumatic event: She had been shopping with her mother and her baby brother, and as they had been standing by the window of a delicatessen, a "human bomb" had detonated, blowing up the entire floor. The mother and brother were killed on the spot. Miri was mainly wounded from the dispersion of glass. Unconscious, she was rushed to the hospital, and it later became clear that she did not remember or realize what had happened. She regained consciousness the following day when she awoke from the operation she had undergone. Miri spent several weeks in the hospital, and it soon became clear that she would not use her voice and that the trauma she had experienced would necessitate a long process of recovery. At that time, she had already been informed as to the death of her mother and baby brother. Her father told me that when the news was broken to her, she did not cry or react.

Why music therapy? Mainly because Miri did not cooperate in verbal therapy, play therapy, or any another art therapy modality. We were not certain that music therapy was the answer, but we decided to give it a try.

Intake and Observation

Miri was brought to therapy by her father, who, in compliance with my request, remained in the room throughout the session. He sat quietly on the couch, watching his little daughter. She would run around the room, not touching any of the musical instruments and not making any reference to her father or to me. Miri could be observed as detached, with the exception of the interest she conveyed through her eyes. I noticed her looking at the guitar, knowing that Miri's mother had loved folk singing and sometimes used to accompany herself on the guitar. I therefore decided not to touch the guitar and to be careful not to rush into too hasty a step. Neither did I talk to her or to her father. The room was quite and calm. Nobody interfered with Miri's walking around. This initial meeting was the experience of three people using their eyes without uttering a sound. The music clinic, which is abundant in instruments from all over the world, cassettes, and a CD library, became a watching room. Nonetheless, I did not feel uncomfortable and neither did Miri's father. We were under the impression that neither did Miri.

According to the model I work with, Developmental-Integrative Model in Music Therapy (Sekeles, 1996), the intake/observation stage holds the potential of turning into the preliminary process of therapy. Consequently, the initial behavior of a client in the music therapy room informs us greatly of stages yet to come far beyond the historical details divulged to us. Therefore, therapeutic considerations must sometimes wait until the scene fills up with meaningful details. In this case: the child before the trauma, the family constellation (relationship with the parents, brothers, grandparents), the child in the educational setting, the community, general development (emotional, sensory-motor, cognitive, social), artistic tendencies, dislikes, and more. It most often takes a considerable amount of time to collect all the details, requiring much patience. Throughout the two weeks of observations (twice a week for a full hour), aspects that had to do with senses, motion, concentration, and tension became more apparent, and Miri was also able to remain in the clinic without her father.

From my observation pages (*ibid.,* Appendix 3, pp. 153–155), I summarized the following aspects (some points were left blank for ethical reasons and others could not yet be examined):

- *Observation location*—Well-equipped music therapy clinic.

- *Duration/date/hour*—

- *Reported to*—

- *Received by*—

- *Name of patient*—Miri (changed for ethical reasons).

- *Age*—4 years old.

- *Address*—

- *Educational framework*—Non-obligatory kindergarten in a city community.

- *Family*—Father and 10-year-old brother. Mother and baby brother were killed two months ago in a terror attack.

- *Reason for referral to music therapy*—Psychological condition of child and muteness after surviving (with comparatively mild physical injuries) the explosion in which her mother and brother were killed; her difficulty to cooperate in verbal therapy and in other tried modalities.

- *Previous and present therapeutic frameworks*—During her hospitalization, the child received psychological aid and occupational therapy. Miri was not able to cooperate.

- *Diagnosis*—Physical injuries were appropriately treated. Her psychological condition remained severe. She does not speak, does not play with the children in kindergarten, barely eats, sleeps about three hours a night, prefers to stay at home in bed, and does not show interest in anything. She moves quietly in the room, does not cry, and scarcely relates to her father and older brother. Miri fits the clinical picture of PTSD.[3]

- *External impression*—Thin little girl, curly blond hair, neatly dressed, cute face, big dark eyes, very sad facial expression, moves nonstop in the room, does not touch anything, and stares around.

- *Equipment employed*—None.

- *Movement* (fine and gross mobility)—Walking and balance looks normal and adequate for her age. Specific motor abilities could not yet be examined.

- *Senses*—What could be examined so far seems normal.

- *Vocality*—Specific vocality could not be examined. The child does not use her voice at all.

- *Rhythmicality*—The present tempo of her walking is pretty fast. Other aspects could not yet be checked.

- *Instrument playing*—She does not touch any musical instrument.

- *Hearing and listening*—Though she does not speak, she seems to listen and understand general directives such as "Please come inside" or "We have finished today, hope to see you next week." I have been told that she has a high level of language comprehension.

- *Emotional aspects*—Miri does not yet initiate contact, but also she does not run away from the music room. She does not express any strong feeling such as anger, fear, aggression, or even passive-aggressiveness. She is mainly passive and receptive only through her eyes and probably her ears. There is no question about the severe psychological damage and the patience required in therapy to hopefully overcome the horrible trauma.

- *Cognitive aspects*—These could not be examined but have been reported to be very good. There is no brain damage.

- *Social aspects*—Cooperation could hardly be examined.

- *Summary and recommendations*—Though Miri shows signs of depression and avoidance of people and almost all everyday functions, she seems to be accepting the music therapy clinic and perhaps the calm atmosphere I try to keep in it. The fact that she gazes at the guitar might help at a proper moment. Patience is always an extremely important aspect in therapy and this is surely so in Miri's case. In the two weeks of observation, she was not pushed to do anything, and we have the impression that it helped her to get used to the room, its physical content, its atmosphere, and probably to the therapist. It also occurs to me that my age may cause Miri to associate me with more of a grandmotherly figure than a (her) mother. This might assist in developing trust.

Therapeutic Considerations: Based on Intake, Practice, and Theory

In the meantime, I had learned that Miri was raised in a warm, loving family. Her father's profession was related to agriculture, her mother's had been in education, and folksinging was a hobby that she took seriously. Grandparents on both sides were still alive and involved in their children's lives. Miri and her brothers had had a good, healthy relationship. Though her father, brother, and grandparents had undergone a horrible experience, they knew that they ought to direct all the efforts toward Miri and were very willing to accept her as she was, not to push her, and to support her with love and care. During this period, her father and brother were supported by a social worker. As for the kindergarten teacher, she was a nice lady who had lost her husband in one of our wars. She therefore treated Miri with patience and took proper caution and care.

Being well aware of the practical and theoretical importance of the preloss human relationship, this background gave me hope. When young children lose a parent before their personality is fully developed and before they fully internalize their parents' image, it is especially necessary to examine the preloss emotional environment and the postloss ability of their surroundings to contain the bereaved child as she is. There is no way to comprehend the change that occurred in the child's behavior without being aware of how she remembers and has internalized the deceased parent. In cases where the parent-child relationship was healthy and facilitating and the surviving parent maintained suitable functioning, though he experienced the loss as well, there is a better chance for the child to adjust and to rebuild her life. Bowlby taught us that it is essential for animals and young children to be close to their mothers in order to physically exist and to mentally construct the representation of the mother's image. In his attachment theory, Bowlby claims that grief indicates the effort of the grieving person to sustain a connection to the dead person. The mandatory departure and the irreversibility of death elicit anxiety and protest. Bowlby (1969, 1973, 1980) wrote three volumes on the subject of loss from the perspective of object relations and the essential role of attachment in development and functioning from infancy to old age. He accentuated the importance of the different stages of mourning: shock and nonacceptance, searching for everything related to the deceased, disintegration of the existing psychological organization, and reorganization. The final stage has to do with the releasing of the bond to the dead person. Kübler-Ross's (1969) stages are as follows: denial and isolation, anger, bargaining, depression, acceptance (pp. 34–122). Though Kübler-Ross discusses work with terminal patients in this book, the stages she formulated are also valid in cases of bereavement.

Miri had gone shopping with her mother and brother and then found herself wounded and in pain in the strange surroundings of a hospital. With her mother suddenly gone, a huge black hole of missing memories enveloped her, but the catastrophic experience was certainly buried somewhere in her brain and heart. This situation struck her with numbness as a radical defense mechanism. We must remember that Miri was merely 4 years old. It took time until her father could tell her about the explosion and loss of her mother and brother. Miri did not actually witness what had happened, but she probably heard it and perhaps some quick flash ran in her mind. The defense mechanism of denial served to hinder the realization of the horrifying events and prevent any possible pain. Smilansky (1981) claims that only at the age of 4 to 5 does the child begin to understand the concept of death. At this stage in life, children conceptualize death as a different form of life, similar to sleep in a way, and thus reversible. The full understanding of what it means to die is delayed to a further stage, which takes place at age 9, 10, or even 11, according to some researchers (pp. 36–37). Smilansky claims that many children in a loss situation are afraid that they may fall asleep and never wake. Perhaps this was partially contributing to Miri's sleeplessness in addition to a more general anxiety as the result of the Post Traumatic Stress Disorder (PTSD).

Miri's father, with whom I regularly met, impressed me with his ability to mobilize his energy for Miri and his 10-year-old son, while still tending to his own mourning process. Though he shared the typical characteristics of Israeli men who served in a selected military group and mostly kept his emotions to himself, in this particular situation he was committed to doing anything for his children. He also amazed me with his understanding that it would be a long process and that he had to trust me to calculate the proper timing to intervene. Intervention, as Bruscia (1998) defines it, is "a purposeful attempt to mitigate an existing condition in order to affect some kind of change" (p. 44). In Miri's case, the intervention began by bringing her to the music therapy clinic where she could soon be left with the therapist. Breznitz (1983), in discussing "the denial of stress," claims that denial works as a barrier between life and death. From this point of view, it denies the psychobiological continuation of life. Not to know and not to touch actually exempt the child from coping with pain and loss and the irreversibility of death.

First Stage

Following an additional week similar in content to the four observational meetings, I had the feeling that a more active intervention could take place: Miri arrived at the clinic, where soft music, lullaby style, welcomed her. In the middle of the room there were some handmade animal puppets and symbolic figures (grandfather, angel, witch, baby, etc.). I sat on the carpet activating the puppets, joining the music, inventing lullaby words, and putting the puppets to sleep on a cushion. Miri watched, stopped moving, suddenly sat near the cushion, and began to slowly move back and forth to the rhythm of the music. I continued to address her, describing what she was doing with new words. At a certain moment, Miri put her head on the carpet near the puppets, closed her eyes, and fell asleep until the end of our meeting.

When Miri's father arrived, she was still asleep. He told me that she was accustomed to going to bed with her mother singing to her. Since her death, when he tried to do the same or to tell her a story, she would pull the blanket over her head, signaling her unwillingness to listen. We both considered her response to the improvised "bedtime story" positive, specifically since calm sleeping was one of the treatment's objectives and it happened in a manner more similar to her normal past. On this occasion, her father told me that Miri loved many Israeli songs and that she even knew very complicated texts and melodies by heart.

In the subsequent meeting, I sat on the carpet holding a soft teddy bear in my arms, singing a Hebrew bear song to him. Again, Miri sat near me and looked at the bear. I handed him to her softly. She took the bear while I continued the song. After half an hour, she placed the bear on the sofa, approached the shelves of recordings, and looked at them intensively. I have about a thousand cassettes as well as CDs, records, and more. The cassettes are organized in different colors. Light blue is the color of the Israeli song cassettes. I pointed at this shelf and told her that she could choose one. Miri hesitated, then randomly removed a cassette and placed it in my hand. I understood this as a request to listen to it and inserted it in the tape recorder. It was the music of Yoni Rechter, one of our talented composers, whose music and harmonization have original features. The first song was titled "The Most Beautiful Girl in the Kindergarten." She could certainly have chosen a different cassette, and it could have been a different song. However, what had happened left me with an elated feeling of "something good is happening with Miri. There is hope."

The following session, Miri brought a CD of Israeli songs, which she was fond of, according to her father. These songs were not meant for children, and the lyrics were not simple. They consisted of a collection of a variety of songs sung by Mati Caspi in his semiapathic poker voice. I could not avoid comparing his expression to hers, which in a way was very similar. Miri stopped walking around and sat near to me on the carpet, leaning against the sofa and listening quietly to the singing. At the end, I decided to softly join in the performer's singing. Miri did not react clearly but stayed in her place.

In this session, we further established the phase of mutual listening, which in music therapy represents the *dynamics of being*. This stage persisted for three months and enabled me to gradually introduce tiny changes: to join in singing to different performers she brought, sometimes adding a small musical instrument, then an autoharp, an alto recorder, and a piano. Following these three months, Miri entered the clinic, went straight to the string instruments (hanging on the wall), and pointed at the guitar. A heart-warming moment resulted: I took the guitar and handed it to her, and she placed it on the carpet.

Therapeutic Considerations

Virtually all of the professional literature dealing with children's conditions resulting from PTSD discusses the importance of gradual intervention; patience; using clear, simple words; emotional reassurance; and behavioral consistency. Specifically, when there is an inhibition of feelings, meaning: no way out, no sharing, no ventilation. Tatelbaum (1984), in her book *The Courage to Grieve,* emphasizes that "the manner of death affects our grief. Sudden death (war, accidents) causes shock, anxiety, distress ..." (p. 14). As Miri had been fixated on this stage, the only way to help her out was to be there with her, encourage tiny variations, and allow her to gradually raise her head above the water.

This is a summary of what happened during the first stage of therapy. Following a lengthy period of mutism and detachment, Miri brought her own familiar, reassuring material (Israeli songs) and used it to connect to the music therapy clinic, to the therapist, to her dead mother, and, above all, to herself. She chose adult and not typical children's songs, most with complicated lyrics and melodies, but they were hers. The Israeli songs, according to my interpretation, were like golden threads connecting her to the beauty and warmth of her mother and enabled her to be aided and comforted by good memories at this stage. So far, selecting the music and bringing it to the clinic was the active part of the music therapy, and the mutual listening was the receptive music therapy. I considered the initiation of the active part an additional step toward normal life.

Second Stage

The guitar was lying on the carpet where Miri had placed it. I softly touched the strings and stopped. Miri then took my hand and pushed it toward the strings.

Each time a new variation transpired, I felt as though it was part of a process of rebirth. The first variation was Miri sitting on the carpet (attention and concentration), the second was Miri sitting on the carpet and moving to the rhythm of the music played (turning the external stimulation into a self-action), the third was choosing a cassette (demonstrating initiation and interest in the music therapy room), the fourth was listening to it (dynamics of "being"), and the fifth was bringing her own cassettes for mutual listening (connecting her home life to the clinic by bringing material of her own). The final variation emerged after three months through a request she made (though had not yet verbally expressed): Play the guitar for me. I quickly screened a proper song and decided in favor of a Mati Kaspi melody with lyrics by Jehonathan Geffen, "A Place for Concern":

> *At the end of the sky and at the end of the desert,*
> *there is a remote place covered with wild flowers.*
> *God sits there, observes, and thinks about his creation.*
> *It is forbidden to pick the flowers of the garden.*
> *And he is worried, he is enormously worried.*
> (1st verse)

My choice was made in Miri's footsteps: She loved the composer (probably because of his voice and calm expression) and was familiar with his songs. I sang it accompanying myself on the guitar. Miri listened with her gaze directed at the wall. I thought that it may have been too intimate for her, but still, she listened attentively.

Following that moment, there transpired a few weeks during which Miri would listen to Israeli songs, which I sang, accompanied by the guitar or piano. From a psychological point of view, listening to live music is certainly different from listening to a recording. The patient-therapist-sound/music relationship elicits closeness or even intimacy. The position among these three elements might be very influential. At this stage, the therapist and the music were in an active position and the patient was in a receptive position, but we were gradually approaching a change in this balance: Miri began to say "Yes" and "No" and took an active role in selecting music. The same process was transpiring at home, where she showed more initiative. The situation concerning eating and sleeping had improved, and there were small signs of positive changes even in her kindergarten. Regarding the everyday therapeutic considerations, I examined the dynamical line and concluded that although progress was slow, there had been no regression and the tempo suited the depth of Miri's psychological damage.

Third Stage

After Miri had already been in music therapy for several months, the following occurred: I considered that she was ready for a more direct step and thus chose a children's song about a family where mother and father are mentioned and sang it accompanying myself on the piano. Miri listened and after one verse joined in singing the song. She knew the words perfectly. I stopped singing while she continued on till its end.

The sound of her voice was an utter surprise, as though a tiny little ray of light had peered through the darkness and modestly brightened the clinic. Miri had a pure voice, very beautiful though not yet daring. Her rhythm was perfect, and she knew all the words. My general impression was that her voice was imprisoned in a spiritual cage waiting for salvation and liberation. This incidence indicated the beginning of a new phase: Miri became active, sang gently, not yet in her full voice, chose Israeli songs, was willing to record her singing and relisten to it, spoke very little, but spontaneously uttered few sentences. Positive development appeared when Miri at times began to object to my suggestions and insisted on her own. I accepted these oppositions as the development of ego strength and trust in the therapist. At a certain point, I considered expanding the improvisational component by instrumental interaction. As common with many children suffering from deep anxiety and disability, Miri feared to show anger, and thus was willing to play on different musical instruments but excluded the big drums. An additional two months transpired before she gradually began to touch the drums and, encouraged by my piano playing, broadened the range of dynamics and tempo. At that time, her verbal communication had improved, though she still did not mention her mother, brother, or explosion.

Compared to the initial static stage, therapy was now steadily progressing, albeit at a very slow tempo. Therapeutically speaking, this is the stage at which we have to be careful not to be tempted to rush the process along. I was aware of this danger and thus proceeded hand-in-hand with Miri. As soon as the instrumental improvisation became a part of our meetings, I demonstrated to Miri, by way of modeling, a few examples of vocal improvisations. My goal was to eventually advance to representation, both instrumentally and vocally.

Representations in music therapy are done in different ways and can contribute to the revelation of frightening issues by presenting them in a symbolic way. For example: representation of key figures (such as family members), of a situation (for example trauma), of a conflict (inter-personal, intrapersonal), and more (Sekeles, 1996, pp. 53–56). Miri was ready to take a new step: She invented a story about a bird's family: female, male, and a little daughter. Miri used various instruments, choosing a different wind instrument for each bird and using the cymbal to represent a black, evil cat, which she added to the scene. She "played" the family and asked me to play the cat on the "flageolet oboe." Within a short period of time, she began to add words to the story and transformed it into a murder scene in which the cat killed the bird's entire family. By choosing animals, Miri was able to approach her own family in a circumventing, symbolic way while still maintaining close contact to reality. After relistening to the recording, she commented very softly: "Like my mother and Ben. Both killed by a dangerous man."

Fourth Stage

Following the utterance of these words and the opening of the shelter in which the horrors were hiding, Miri gained the courage for more and more expression through music, words, role playing, and more. The sessions had their own architecture, meaning that they became structured from within: Miri always brought a CD of Israeli songs or chose one from my collection, usually joining the music with her own voice, adding musical instruments. After this opening, which served as a holding frame, she would invent a story on varying subjects, mainly horrifying, including a variety of emotions: anger, sadness, hatred, and aggressiveness. These were mainly directed at "the bad people" or the "bad man" and at times toward her mother. Gradually, she could clearly state that mother left her and took her baby brother with her. For this, she was very angry. Moreover, she told a story in which people were killed by a bomb, disintegrated into tiny pieces, and disappeared forever in the sea. Fifteen years later, I heard of the same image from another little girl whose mother was killed by the collapsing of a floor, and though her father had told her exactly what had happened, she still had the notion that it was just like the explosion of the space shuttle *Columbia.* It taught me that the burden of a horrible blocked image (which, though repressed, does not lose vitality, threatens to surface, and requires much energy to be kept repressed) can be very dangerous and that artistic expression is not always enough. It certainly requires, if possible, a verbal elaboration as well. Indeed, her stories gave us the opportunity to openly discuss the death of her mother and baby brother, ventilate the nightmares, and gradually understand the irreversibility of death.

Fifth Stage

After the ninth month, Miri was able to visit the kindergarten on a regular basis, communicated with her friends there, became manageable at home, joined the family on weekend journeys, could sit with her father and older brother and look at a family album, and slept and ate normally. I remained concerned due to the fact that she cried very little, as if some parts in her being had not really healed. She continued to come to music therapy for an additional year, until at the age of 6 we were certain that she was prepared to proceed to elementary school. That final year, Miri composed about 20 songs, complete with lyrics, through which meaningful and threatening material emerged. She improvised the lyrics and the melody, we recorded them, and I wrote them down in her book. When we terminated therapy, she did not request permission to obtain the book. On the contrary, she said: "This belongs to this room and I want to leave it here."

In the last month of therapy, with permission from the family, we visited the mother's and brother's graves. Miri's father accompanied her, and I brought the guitar along with me. At that time, the graves were covered with plants and flowers. As we sat by the grave, Miri's father uttered a few calming words to her, and Miri said, "Ima [Mother] and Ben live in a nice field with flowers. I want to sing a song for them." Miri sang a well-known Israeli lullaby-style song accompanied by the guitar, and she then burst into an ocean of tears. It was the heaviest cry of her mourning process. We allowed her to cry for a long time, cradled in father's arms. Heeding my recommendation, her father again visited the grave with his two children a week later, after which Miri began participating in all the yearly memorial days.[4] It is important to remember that Miri began the process as a 4-year-old girl and completed music therapy at the age of nearly 6. During this time, she grew up and her understanding of the concept of death changed, and she became better prepared for life.

In his article "Children in Stress Situations," Noah Milgram

(2000), while writing on principles of treatment, warns adults to be careful of forcing their own anxieties and concerns on the children. He recommends surrounding the traumatized child with warm support and confident guidance to help gradually change the fantasies into reality, which is less frightening. I again wish to remind the reader that when the parent or parents support the therapy and cooperate with the therapist, the healing prospect of their child increases. Among other reasons, I included this chapter due to the fact that this was a healthy family constellation, which proved to bear a most positive influence on the process Miri underwent.

SUMMARY

In this chapter, I described and analyzed the process that Miri, a little 4-year-old girl, underwent in 21 months of music therapy. She came to therapy two months after being wounded in a terror attack, in which her mother and baby brother were killed. She suffered from PTSD, stopped talking, became very passive, did not cooperate in kindergarten, ate very little, and had sleeping difficulties.

In spite of the extreme grief and mourning, Miri's family was very cooperative, a fact that contributed tremendously to the therapeutic process. This was especially important since the situation required us to be very patient and not hasten progress before time allowed it. Miri's mother's hobby was singing Israeli songs while accompanying herself on the guitar. Indeed, at the observation stage, the only musical instrument she gazed at was the guitar. Later on, when she progressed and passed the passive stage, the first two actions she took were related to Israeli songs and to the guitar.

Miri passed through five stages of slow, gradual development. Each opened a new, meaningful window to an improved horizon and to the discovery of another hidden layer. After nine months, Miri was able to function at home, in kindergarten, and in the clinic without the anxiety that had stunted her normal development. She could face the facts of loss, reintegrated within the family framework and kindergarten, and expressed herself verbally and musically. She remained in music therapy an additional year to make certain that she went through all the bereavement stages and would be able to cope with elementary school. Miri had a very good background, which, in spite of the horrible trauma, assisted her in returning to life.

The role of the therapist was to walk with her slowly, at her own tempo and ability, along the thorny path of blocked emotions and help her rediscover her voice. The role of the Israeli songs was to connect her to her deceased mother even before she would utter the word "mother" and to support her through well-known and beloved musical material. The role of instrumental and later of vocal improvisations was to facilitate her with the ability to represent figures and situations in a symbolic way, as a circumventing stage, before linking them to reality (concerning improvisation, see Wigram, 2004). The songs Miri created in the fifth stage of music therapy expressed issues from the entire therapeutic period and operated as assurance as to her ego strength.

In his article "Models of Understanding the Reaction to Trauma in Supporting and Defining the Principles of Treating Trauma and Post-trauma," Shabtai Noy (2000) claims that dissociation is important in preventing pain and is therefore important for adjustment. Without the ability to detach from the trauma, the survivor might be overwhelmed with endless anxiety. The treatment teaches the patient to use the dissociation to gradually gain mastery over his life and cope with reality (chapter 2). In Miri's case, she had needed to dissociate herself from the very blurred reality of the explosion in order to eventually be able to emotionally and cognitively reconnect. The DIMT model with which I work considers what may be called pathological symptoms to actually be coping mechanisms. Their eradication is therefore not sufficient.

Another challenge is that of the therapist to remain tolerant of these symptoms as much as is necessary and to assist the family to do the same. Further, the therapist must keep the surviving family member, in this case the father, involved as a protector of the child and as a strong, supporting figure, and take care that the child doesn't develop a dependency on the therapist. Some psychological theories concerning intervention in a situation of uni-occurrence trauma recommend a short therapeutic process that relays a message of health to the parent and to the child (Peterson, Prout, & Schwartz, 1991). In Miri's case, it was not possible to rush the dynamics of the events, but the fact that the music therapy clinic looked like a magic room with many interesting objects and sounds helped to turn it (as far as Miri and her father were concerned) into a nonthreatening space and through this enabled a degree of much needed relaxation.

The closure of the process was the visit to the cemetery in which I took care to be involved as the music therapist and not as a mother figure. The role of the father was very clear, and he acted as the main figure, strong and facilitating.

Many years have passed since Miri's music therapy sessions have ceased, and thanks to her family and to her, I was granted the opportunity to follow up on her development. After finishing high school, she insisted on joining the Israeli army (though she could have obtained an exemption). She coped very well with her duties, completed her service, and began her academic studies at one of our universities. Noy (2000) said: "Grief is boundless, but a person learns to distance it, as he does with some other feelings, thus preventing them from overwhelming him" (p. 72).

Notes

(1) The song was written by M. Shelem, a shepherd and musician, after two of his fellow shepherd friends were ambushed and murdered in 1937 by Arab terrorists. In 1936, the opposition of the Arabs began to take the form of armed insurrection, and the Israelis responded with retaliation. This was one of the more horrific periods of violence in the country.

(2) Amos Fink was killed by a sniper in July 1948 during a period of ceasefire. Amos was a lover of nature and a soldier in the Jewish Brigade during World War II, after which he volunteered to help survivors immigrate to Israel. He served as a lieutenant during the Israeli Independence War. Amos left behind a two-month-old baby, Tamar, and a young widow, my eldest sister.

(3) Post Traumatic Stress Disorder (PTSD) "is an anxiety disorder arising as a delayed and protracted response after experiencing or witnessing a traumatic event involving actual or threatened death or serious injury to self or others." (Colman, 2001, p. 572). The symptoms include a numbing of responsiveness and eating and sleeping problems, which typified Miri's condition.

(4) In the Jewish tradition, every moment is detailed and ritualized, beginning with the prayer of confession (Vidui), continuing with the

laws concerning the body, and concluding with the burial procedures and mourning practices (seven consecutive days, then the 30th day following the burial and each Memorial Day). This ritualization provides everyone involved with a firm structure that enables the mourners to focus on their grief and places the burden of the organizational details on the community (cooking, cleaning, participating, and paying last respects, which is perceived in Judaism as the "truest act of charity"). The burial customs are rooted in the biblical era. From an emotional point of view, these customs and the gradual process through which they are observed hold exceptional psychological wisdom. Statistically, 86% of the Jewish citizens in Israel (religious and secular) practice these customs (Faber & Tur-Paz, 2006).

Chapter Two

THE ROLE OF ISRAELI SONGS IN COPING WITH COLLECTIVE AND PERSONAL GRIEF

"The best way to get to know any bunch of people is
to go and listen to their music."
(Woody Guthrie, 1975)

Dedicated to Chana Zinder[1]

INTRODUCTION

In the first chapter, I presented a case description and analysis of music therapy with a traumatized young child, Miri, who brought Israeli songs of her choice to the sessions. She initially used them receptively and later actively.

In this second chapter, I deal with phenomena that seem to be most prominent in Israeli culture: Israeli songs. In order to understand their role in life and in music therapy, I will first present a short description of their background and its significance in their development.

For many years, ethnomusicologists debated over the definition of songs created in modern Israel. The fact that the state of Israel is young (declared independent in 1948) made it difficult to define the birth date of the Israeli song and define its parametrical qualities. Is an "Israeli song" every song ever written in Hebrew? Is it every song composed in Israel? Nowadays, the definition has been broadened and the tendency is to define Israeli songs (or Hebrew songs or semi–folk songs) as those created in Israel since the very beginning of the national movement in the 19th century and until today. In 1993, Hanoch Ron described this occurrence as being "In constant search of a musical identity" (pp. 21–24). Ron claims that Israeli songs represent multicultural aspects: personal expression mixed with the wish to be detached from the collective influence of the Diaspora. He emphasizes the constant struggle between the Oriental features (unisono and melismatic texture) and western ones (harmony and melodic lines). He also accentuates the desire they portray to return to nature, to revive biblical texts, and to overcome the difficulties of the Hebrew language (the accents and the quality of sound) through music. Ron describes the development of our songs as a main road from which smaller branches stretch out, and Eliram (2002) stresses the eclecticism that typifies our songs.

Concerning the specific topic of this chapter, historically speaking, this current period (since the 19th century) covers many important events and national traumas experienced by the Jewish people. This includes World War II and the postwar immigrations, which brought multicultural groups from all over the world to the country. Due to this, there exists a rich collection of folk songs in Israel developed in the Diaspora and brought to Israel through different ethnic immigration groups. Such are the Jewish folk songs in Yiddish, Ladino, Moroccan, Yemenite, Russian, Amharic, English, and other languages. Some songs remained as they were in their original language, while others were translated into Hebrew. At times, themes were taken and integrated within the new musical culture. (See also Gradenwitz, 1996, on the music of Israel from the biblical era to modern times.)

Israeli songs very clearly reflect the development and concerns of the country: the establishment of a normal society that exerts itself through agriculture, industry, cultural integration, revival of the ancient Hebrew language, and the crystallization of Hebrew education and culture. In her book *The Early Hebrew Folksong,* Yael Reshef (2004) accentuates the fact that our songs were and are sung in the community and in the Hebrew language, as well as were and are a part of the national establishment of a new society (chapter 2).

Israel was declared a state in 1948. Subsequently, the Arabs' continuous attacks against Israel, supported by the surrounding Arab countries, developed into a global war. The tension between the sides and the acts of terror have persisted throughout the years before, in between, and after the different wars between Israel and the Arab countries. This continuous stressful situation led to a complicated emotional state: pain, grief, hatred, anxiety, inside and outside conflicts, suspicion and difficulty in trusting others, and, above all, the desire for peace. One might say that the entire establishment of Israel is accompanied by the need to "survive and create life in spite of the difficulties, and to defeat death, though it thrashes again and again at our open wounds."

It is important to emphasize the fact that each side of the conflict in the Middle East is continuously suffering. Sentiments similar to the ones presented here are likewise voiced by the Palestinian side. Death and anxiety exceed mentalities, and the fact is that the entire region is busy with simply surviving, though each party maintains its own beliefs, ideology, morality, and coping strategies.

We discover at an early stage in therapy that there are deep layers of anxiety and lack of self-confidence beneath the surface of everyday life. This became very clear to me when I volunteered to do music therapy with a mixed group of Israeli Jews and Israeli Arabs (Sekeles, 2005a). Generally speaking, the dangers remained throughout the years, with changing variations. In the 1930s, our parents did not allow us to walk freely in certain places even near our home. Since the age of 3, pictures of a terrorist butchering a neighboring family with a knife have accompanied me. Since the 1960s, our children have not been allowed to pick up unknown objects from the ground because of the lingering danger of "finger mines." These days, our grandchildren must be careful not to spend their time in crowded places, shopping centers, etc., due to the threat of "human bombs." As I emphasized in the first chapter, it is nearly impossible to cope with death caused by terror and even more so when it comes to the death of children. To remain optimistic and to strive for a peaceful, normal life is a necessary longing and should be the main ideal underlined in Israeli education. I would hope this to be true in Palestinian education as well. (For complementary reading, see Bard, 2006.)

This is neither a political essay nor a historical one. Therefore, I am not presenting an organized lecture on the Israeli-Palestinian conflict. Through this very short introduction, I have attempted to present a description of the background in which people in Israel live and in which songs were and are created.

Israeli Songs

Natan Shahar (1999) pinpointed 1895 as the year in which the first book of Israeli songs was published. This was followed by hundreds of songbooks promoted by the authorities and distributed for communal use

(p. 497). These included the creation of songs for children from an early age on (Gal-Pe'er, 1978, pp. 3–17). As aforementioned, the songs became an important tool for developing and reviving the modern Hebrew language and the material of social integration and emotional cohesion. As Israel had many composers who immigrated from different cultures, it is interesting to observe how, for example, musicians from Western Europe intentionally composed songs with Oriental motives, thus creating a new integration between the East and West. This integration can also be observed through the subjects and texts: camels, desert, shepherds, landscape, etc., which were certainly a far cry from the world of Chaim Alexander, a German Jew from Berlin[2] or Paul Ben Chaim from Munich[3] or Marc Lavri from Latvia[4] with first-rate classical education. It should also be mentioned that there are musical groups and individual performers in Israel who try to collaborate with Arab musicians and others in order to create a new integration. Examples: Habreira Hativyit ("The Natural Selection") is a mixed group initiated by the singer-drummer Shlomo Bar, born in Morocco and reviving his own tradition in an individual way; Alei Hazayit ("The Olive Leaves" group); Bustan Avraham ("The Garden of Abraham" group); Yair Dalal, the oud player who spent time playing and absorbing the music of the Azazme Beduin tribe in Israel's southern Negev and in Sinai; and Tsippi Fleischer, a composer who invested a lot of effort in research and in composing integrated Arabic-Western music. I would like to clarify that the abovementioned examples are but a few among a long list of creators of music.

Israeli songs did and still do play an integral part in various occasions:

- Working situations[5]
- Educational settings[6]
- Personal and community assemblies[7]
- Youth Movement activities[8]
- Different rituals, including grief and mourning situations[9]
- Folk dances[10]
- Group and individual music therapy settings[11]

Throughout the years, there grew a nucleus of composers-poets-singers of songs who became very well known and appreciated for their specific contribution to the community and its individuals. To mention a few examples: Matityahu Shelem, who was born in 1904 in Poland and immigrated to Israel in 1921, was a kibbutz member and a shepherd. Shelem did not study music until later in his life. He used to compose his songs and let another musician (Yehuda Sharet) write them down. His songs are saturated with the smell of landscapes, agriculture, and a healthy new spirit. From this point of view, he can be titled a composer who represents the agricultural community.[12] Neomi Shemer, born in 1930 in a kibbutz, mostly wrote the music and the lyrics to her songs based on a broad knowledge of Jewish history. She won The Israeli Prize in 1987 for her contribution to the field of the Hebrew song (Miron, 1987). She died in 2004.[13] Arik Einstein represents another area in folk music, a mixture of the traditional idealistic Israel with a new pop-rock style.[14]

Alongside all these, there also developed an Oriental style of composers and singers born and raised in families originating in the Arabic-speaking countries. In their songs, we can hear the typical Middle Eastern–ornamented melodies sometimes integrated with Western character. From a textual point of view, among other subjects they deal with the difficulties encountered by the Oriental society as immigrants in Israel. These mainly included discrimination, economic hardship, desperation, and disappointment when their dreams met reality. One of the most renowned people in fighting and demanding official recognition of the Oriental–Middle Eastern musical style is Avihu Medina. Medina was born to Yemenite parents who immigrated to Israel in the first quarter of the 20th century. He is a poet, musician, and singer; has won many awards in Israel; and in 1995 was declared by the Smithsonian Institute as the representative of Israeli folk songs.[15] Shoshana Damari, "the queen of the Israeli song," was born in Yemen in 1923 and immigrated to Israel in 1924 with her parents. Damari had a distinctive alto voice with a strong Yemenite accent and unusual dynamical and diapasonic abilities. She collaborated for many years with the poet Natan Alterman and the musician Moshe Vilenski, who often arranged her songs for a full orchestra. In 1988, she won The Israel Prize for lifelong enterprise. Damari died in 2006.[16]

The abovementioned figures represent merely a partial list of examples from a large selection of excellent poets-musicians-performers who create in the country.

Remembrance Days

There are many remembrance days in Israel, including those for World War II, Independence Day, for different wars, for the murder of Prime Minister Rabin, and more. Throughout each of these days, including during the invariable ceremonies, the Israeli radio and television broadcast songs, history, and more. Over the past 10 years, I have collected these songs and found that they can be organized into the following categories:

A Personal Loss

For example, "My Young Brother Yehuda" was written (with music by Yochanan Zarai) by Ehud Manor about his brother, who lost his life in the War of Attrition:

> *My young brother Yehuda, do you hear? do you know?*
> *The Sun still rises every morning and its light is white*
> *and in the evening the wind scatters the leaves of the garden.*
> *The first rain came down two days ago on Tuesday evening,*
> *and the sky is visible again in the puddle on the main road.*
> (1st verse)

The theme of "death has taken you but the world did not change and life goes on" is recognized by the literature on death and grief (Rubin, 1990; Aldridge, 1998b; Schneider, 2003; Grant, 2005). Perhaps this is the strongest connection between death and life, the fact that people cope and survive simply because life goes on. Through the questionnaires (see pages 26–27), I have learned that for people who have lost family members and friends through wars and terror, these types of personal songs revive the pain and grief. For some, they function as part of an individual lamentation.

Songs Describing Situations, Relationship, Places

Another section of songs illustrates certain *situations during war* and describes places, warriors, friendships, and more. Many of these songs are calm, sad, minor, and not heroic as one might expect. Example: "Hareut" ("Friendship"), lyrics by Chaim Guri, music by Sasha Argov:

> *On the Negev descends the fall night*
> *and lights up the stars very quietly.*
> *When the wind crosses on the porch*
> *clouds are walking on the road.*
> *Already a year.*
> *We almost have not felt*
> *how the times have passed in our fields.*
> *Already a year and there are few of us left*
> *So many are no longer among us.*
> (1st verse)

This serene song is about warriors' friendship and the longing for lost togetherness, which was signed in blood. The music softens the song, develops slowly from the diapason and dynamical point of view, and closes quietly.

Nostalgic Songs

These songs describe a better world of peaceful life. A kind of pictorial, rustic art, they serve as a source for indulging in wishful thinking in a chaotic existence of constant death and grief. For example, "We Are From the Same Village," lyrics and music by Neomi Shemer:

> *We are both from the same village*
> *The same height, the same forelock,*
> *The same clipped speech.*
> *What is there to say?*
> *For we are from the same village.*
> Chorus:
> *And on Friday evenings*
> *When a soft breeze passes through the black treetops*
> *I remember you.*
> (1st verse)

Israel is a very small country. People often know each other, certainly those of the same age and generation, school, youth movement, village, or army unit. Thus, the personal grief often turns to a communal pain. In addition, when a well-known person is killed, as in the case of Prime Minister Rabin, the lamentations of thousands of very young people, flooding the place with flowers, candles, and gentle singing, demonstrate the great need of people in this country to express their repressed anxiety. They make use of official public opportunity to convey their own, personal pain.

Songs of Beautiful Israel

These songs express love for the country, its landscape, and nature, but again in a calm, romantic fashion and by no means in a heroic style. I believe that the calm, soft, sometimes cradlelike songs help people to identify with the collective pain and cope with personal grief. Heroic songs may be appropriate for military marches or for encouragement (as was done on the Egyptian radio during wars) but not for mourning situations, unless the anger involved is unbearable and must be expressed vigorously.

Songs of Peace

These describe the longing for peace and the desire to end all wars and killing. One example is "Peace on Israel," lyrics by David Barak, music by Efi Netzer:

> *If peace will come tomorrow*
> *To every generation*
> *From the Heights to Mt. Nevo will glow*
> *The bonfires in creation*
> *From mount to mount they'll peace proclaim*
> *And a great light will swell*
> *When new day dawns in tomorrow's frame*
> *On all of Israel.*
> Refrain: *Peace, peace*
> (Last verse)

Most peace songs bear a merry, rhythmical style, and at least part of them (mostly in the refrain) widen the range of voice and dynamics. These are songs of encouragement and provide hope for a new future. They are predominantly performed on Independence Day, which follows the day of commemoration for the soldiers who have fallen in wars.

Holocaust Songs

During the memorial day for the Holocaust, we hear many songs that were composed during World War II in concentration camps, ghettos, and elsewhere. These are Holocaust songs sung in Yiddish and in Hebrew (Sapoznik, 1999).

Mourners' Songs

These songs are performed in cemeteries in Israel over the graves of the deceased by special lamenting women, mainly of Oriental origin. The prayer El Male Rahamim (Merciful God) is also sung in funerals and on memorial days. Furthermore, it is not customary to perform music in cemeteries, though some communities have begun to do so as an addition to the usual ceremony.

All of these categories contribute to a massive collection of songs incessantly played throughout our memorial days. I therefore decided to gather information on the influence of the songs on different people: I asked 100 people several questions, via electronic mail, concerning the personal influence the songs heard during our memorial days had on them. I also included questions about their most beloved songs, poets, and composers. The group included religious and secular people of ages 10 to 70, from Western and Oriental origins. Seventy-one people said that they could not avoid listening to the songs during these days. Ten said that since the songs are so sad, beautiful, and nostalgic, they ignite in them pride for the country and its artists. Nine admitted that they couldn't stand the music, as it compelled them "to remember" and that they were angry at the authorities for the "brainwashing" and manipulation generated through the songs. One person said: "I want to grieve when it comes, I do not want to be part of a grieving public and to be told what to do. The songs are mostly marvelous, but this is exactly their danger. The threat of addiction." A young religious woman said: "I can hear the same songs during the year, but only during the memorial

days do I feel that they have a deep, internal place within my being."
Two children (ages 11 and 12) said that the songs make them feel like
the grown-ups. Three said that this is the best part of our heritage, and
three refused to answer. As for the most influential song, more than half
(ages 12 to 35) referred to "The Little Prince," lyrics by Jehonathan
Gefen, music by Shem Tov Levi:

> *The little prince from B group*
> *will never see a sheep eating a flower*
> *and all the roses are thorns now*
> *as his little heart became a frozen ice.*
> (Refrain)

The other half of the group questioned chose differently, though almost
all chose well-known artists. Even those who disliked the entire idea
made the same choices: Arik Einstein, Neomi Shemer, Sasha Argov,
Chava Alberstein, and Yoni Rechter (some of these are the writers of
both the lyrics and the music). The poets chosen were Natan Altermann,
Lea Goldberg, Natan Jeonatan, Rachel, Ehud Manor, Yoram Tehar-Lev
(none of these are from a young generation). Some children did not know
the names of poets or composers, but they did recognize singers. I did
not ask patients, but from practice I know that many patients who do not
like to listen to the abovementioned categories suffer from drug
addiction. The material they prefer is trance music and "Dici"
(depressive) songs. These patients also admitted that the memorial days
are of no interest to them. Other patients preferred Israeli songs and used
them for different reasons (see also note 11):

- To identify with the song (lyrics and music)
- To use it as a starting point for active singing and verbal
- communication
- To use it as a symbol and to circumvent direct speech
- As a basis for musical, movemental, and verbal
  improvisation
- As artistic material that helps relive and recall painful
- memories
- As an inspiration that encourages the personal writing of
  songs

SUMMARY

This chapter focused on the role of Israeli songs in coping with collective and personal grief. In order to clarify the nature of this particular function, I included a short description of the historical background from which the growth and development of Israeli songs emerged. I thought it very important to accentuate the influence of the immigration of musicians on the special character of the songs, the general role of the songs in the new Israeli community and in the renewal of the ancient Hebrew language, and the integration of the East and West and their impact on the emotional state of the inhabitants. The anxiety, anger, grief, continuous tension, and loss of people in terror attacks and in wars all necessitate spiritual strength and the ability to sustain hope and belief. The fact that individuals, communities, and authorities use Israeli songs in bereavement situations bears evidence to the great importance given to the music and to the words. The significance of the songs in memorial days is obvious from kindergarten on. The results of the questionnaire I distributed to 100 people showed that most found consolation in the soft, nostalgic music as opposed to music bearing a more heroic nature. This music helps connect inwardly to our community, to the bereaved parents, brothers, wives, husbands, and friends, and to our Self. Both listening (a receptive situation) and singing (an active situation) contribute and influence people. Listening and singing are actions regularly done in Israel and make it possible to identify with the collective grief while remaining with one's own personal grief.

It was very difficult to choose a small number of artists (poets, musicians, and performers) as representatives of the different issues I conveyed. The list merely functions to exemplify the subject, and different representatives could very easily have been chosen. I faced the same problem in chapter 5, and the only way to deal with it was to make a personal decision and to follow it. Another question relates to the translations from Hebrew to English. Since these are two completely different linguistic systems, it is very difficult to remain true to the intonation and symbolic descriptions inherent in the songs.

Music is an auditory experience, and the emotional significance of songs can most accurately be conveyed by actually listening to the music itself. The disc enclosed will help the reader to better appreciate this chapter's nature and the emotional character of the songs discussed.

Notes

(1) Chana Zinder was a physiotherapist, dance therapist and expert in treating pain. We were very close colleagues and friends for over 30 years of therapeutic development, until her death in October 1990. Chana taught me the meaning of therapeutic faithfulness and of ethical integrity.

(2) Chaim Alexander was born in Berlin (1915) and immigrated to Israel in 1936. He was a composer, pianist, and teacher at the Rubin Academy of Music. Among his many activities, he wrote beautiful vocal arrangements for Israeli songs' choruses.

(3) Paul Ben Chaim was born in Munich (1897). He was Bruno Walter's assistant in Germany and immigrated to Israel in 1933. In his Israeli composition and "folk songs," he used Middle Eastern overtones and Oriental themes. (See also Hirshberg, 1990.)

(4) Marc Lavri was born in Riga, Latvia (1903) and died in Israel in 1967. He was well known for his romantic-idealistic love for the country, which was reflected in his musical creativity and in the themes he chose for his compositions. He also incorporated texts of many prominent poets or traditional material and wrote music to them. One of his most celebrated songs, known throughout the world, is "Hava Nagila" ("Let Us Rejoice"; lyrics: Idelshon). Lavry introduced his arrangements to songs to the concerts halls of Israel and was also an enthusiastic supervisor of music education in the Israeli Ministry of Education and Culture.

(5) Israeli songs describe different work situations and were also sung during work. My father, who was a pioneer at the beginning of the 20th century, told us that they used to sing Israeli songs (and to sometimes create them) for self-encouragement and to promote group identity.

(6) Songs for children nearly did not exist; thus they had to be composed. The general inclination was to speak and sing in Hebrew. This ideology prevented parents and teachers (if they were new immigrants) from singing to the children in other languages. Some creators, such as Levin Kipnis, devoted themselves to this task and wrote rich collections of

children's lyrics (Hacohen, 1982).

(7) Group singing in the community is very popular in Israel and has actually gained new momentum in recent years. People sing at different times: birthday parties, army gatherings, Independence Day, school events, holidays, and more. In addition, there are specific assemblies announced for the public, dedicated to folksinging with musical accompaniment and guiders. It should also be mentioned that army entertainment groups and bands are an important source for songwriters; in their performances, they spread songs all over the country.

(8) There are many youth movements in Israel in which singing and folk dancing have important roles. This is true in youth movements of different ideologies and beliefs.

(9) Singing plays an important role in all the ceremonies, official and unofficial, and specifically in the ceremonies that were established during our days of mourning. Choirs and soloists have an appointed place and timing, which contributes a familiar psychological frame to the event.

(10) Folk dances in Israel are deeply related to the Israeli songs, and many of them were born due to collaboration between composers and dance choreographers. There exist folk dances arranged to a certain song and also the opposite, songs composed to accompany dances. Israeli folk dances passed through a similar process as the songs. Gurit Kadman, who was a pioneer in the field, defined folk dances in the following way: "A folk dance is a dance that has been created by the people for the people, and a large part of the public should be dancing it" (personal knowledge).

(11) In music therapy, we often use Israeli songs both in group settings (Amir, 1998; Wiess, 2004) and in individual therapy, as was demonstrated in the first chapter. It was found to be especially effective with groups in psychiatry (see chapter 9), including closed wards. The shared singing experience promotes a feeling of community, helps to choose and elicit subjects for elaboration, connects to normal reality, helps celebrate different events, and elevates mood.

(12) Example: *Matityahu Shelem Songs: Shibolet Basade*. CD. Akum. The Company of Traditional Hebrew Song. 2004.

(13) Example: *Neomi Shemer's Achar Katzir (After Harvest)*. G-035 (b). Hed Arzi CD. 105 (2004). Givatron Vocal Company.

(14) Example: *Arik Einstein: The Best*. CD. NMC, Israel Music Com. (2003). Arik Einstein composed and sings.

(15) Example: *Avihu Medina: No Rest*. CD. AML Production, Israel Music Com. (2004). Avihu Medina composed and sings.

(16) Example: *Shoshana Damari: Israeli, Yemenite, and Other Folksongs*. CD. Vanguard Classics. 6025 BOOOOO23E9. (1995). Damari sings.

Chapter Three

THE COURAGE TO DIE: NATHANIEL, A TERMINAL CANCER PATIENT

A CASE ANALYSIS

"We are not condemned to meet death with empty hands.
To begin with, we have to find a meaning in our life."
(Sogyal Rinpoche, 1993, *The Tibetan Book of Living and Dying*)

Dedicated to Dr. Jaacov Avni and Dr. Alma Avni[1]

INTRODUCTION

"After receiving my diagnosis, I was shocked. I could not react. I could not discuss it with my wife and children. I had nightmares and daytime horror-fantasies in which I could see the cancer cells moving from my lungs, creating settlements everywhere, becoming larger and larger. Then, suddenly, a huge vacuum cleaner entered my blood vessels and sucked up all the malignant cells as well as all my internal organs, till I was left empty, clean, and dead."

Nathaniel told of this dream (or perhaps fantasy) when he was first introduced to music therapy by his oncologist. She had given consideration to the fact that he had loved music since childhood, played the French horn in his free time, and participated in an amateur orchestra. Nathaniel had finished high school (specializing in natural science), the army (prestigious unit), and university (majoring in natural science). He was married, with four children; had a job in science; and, in addition, showed impressive personal development. Then, at the age of 45, he began to cough heavily and had some shortness of breath and bronchitis. He was sent for medical examinations and was found to suffer from lung cancer.

Nathaniel was an emotionally and physically healthy person. He had smoked heavily from age 17, but like many others had not considered the possible consequences. He had fairly good knowledge of medical issues and seemed to be emotionally capable of confronting the bad news. In reality, he was shocked to hear the news from the oncologist and had responded by isolating himself in his room for a few days. After a while, he was able to collect himself and collaborate with the specialist and with his family. Meanwhile, his wife had difficulties digesting the bitter pill and explaining it to the children (ages 10, 14, 16, and 20). The medical team at the hospital clinic (physician, nurses, social worker, and psychologist) was of great help, and the family, supported by Nathaniel himself, found the courage and the means to deal and cope with the situation. It is important to mention that compared to doctors who commonly used standard distancing techniques and tactics to cope with the emotional burden of treating the terminally ill (Maguire, 1985), Nathaniel was fortunate to have an empathic oncologist who knew how to talk to him in a straightforward manner. She informed him of his illness, though in those years doctors preferred to conceal the truth from their patients (Buckman, 1996).

Nathaniel was referred to music therapy following a few months of chemotherapy, after his condition had deteriorated and it was clear that a metastatic process was already active. In accordance with the family's request, he was sent home to spend his last weeks/months in a supporting, loving environment.[2] Backer, Hannon, and Gregg (1994) discuss the desire of many patients to return home and die there. They mention the difficulties in executing this wish, such as the family's exhaustion of physical and emotional energy, financial problems, and more (pp. 60–62). In addition, due to the intimate and intensive situation at home, a severe illness, in this case terminal, might arouse all sorts of unfinished business and conflicts. To treat a person in an optimal way requires a lot of patience, calmness, a systematic approach, courage, and, above all, love. Nathaniel's family decided to do their best. They had the support of the medical fund, they had each other, and they had friends who were able and willing to help.

As abovementioned, music therapy commenced by the oncologist's recommendation and was administered at the patient's home on a private basis, with some financial support from the medical fund. Due to Nathaniel's condition, it was obvious that the approach should focus on receptive music therapy in which most of the work is done through the patient listening to music and not by creating the music as is done in active music therapy. In receptive therapy, the listening material is played according to the patient's choice and request. For example:

- Precomposed music played by a tape recorder (cassette, CD, records).
- Precomposed music performed by the therapist.
- Music improvised by the therapist.
- Music and fantasizing.
- Music and reading poetry or reacting with movement or painting.
- Music accompanying the last moments of life.

The music therapy sessions continued for four months, mostly twice a week in the patient's home, up until his death. Additional music was performed at the graveyard during the ceremony of the 30th day.[3] This was done in accordance with Nathaniel's request. As aforementioned in the first chapter, during the past years, many families have chosen to sing or play music at the burial ceremony and on the forthcoming traditional days. Nathaniel planned it in advance, and I had to promise him to honor his request.

THE MEANING OF MUSIC IN NATHANIEL'S LIFE

First Meeting

In the first meeting, I already knew several details: the medical condition, the treatment and Nathaniel's perspective; his musical background; his life history; the family constellation; the physical space in which we would spend the music therapy sessions; and some theoretical and practical ideas concerning music therapy with terminal cancer patients.

When I first entered Nathaniel's house, I saw him sitting on an armchair in a spacious area, flowers on the table, a black upright German piano in the corner, shelves with books and cassettes, a good-quality tape recorder, and a window facing a small, lovely garden. Nathaniel was a tall man, very thin at that stage, pale, breathing somewhat heavily, not very talkative—but the expression in his black eyes was welcoming. The suggestion of music therapy had come from his physician, but he had willingly agreed to try it.

I presented myself shortly and told him that the path we would take would be in accordance with his wishes and needs. "Good," Nathaniel had responded. He showed me his recorded music collection, and it was clear that he liked instrumental and vocal compositions from the Renaissance to the Romantic era. I wondered if he disliked music of the 20th century. However, this was not the immediate issue at hand. He told me of his instrument playing, admitting that he had had to quit because of his breathing problems.[4]

Though Nathaniel could still speak at that stage, use his hands, walk, eat alone, etc., he quickly tired and clearly stated that he would prefer to listen to music rather than do something active. He asked me if I would play the piano for him, and I agreed. During this initial meeting, his illness was mentioned through the nightmare he described, but he did not want to talk about it any further, and the general feeling was one of "he is examining me." Half an hour went by, and we were still conversing on different subjects concerning his work, his family (I had met only his wife), and specifically his children. He very much wanted me to meet his children, and I promised to do so as soon as possible. Before leaving, I asked his permission to try the piano. He willingly agreed, and I played Schumann's "Dreaming" ("Träumerei"), which is short and calm. He thanked me and we parted. When I stood at the door, he said: "Next time, please bring me music of your choice that I probably do not know." I promised I would.

Therapeutic Considerations

After becoming aware of my personal feelings concerning this first meeting and linking them to my general approach to death and dying, I was more prepared to think about the possible therapeutic process. The use of receptive musical experiencing is completely legitimate in music therapy and is not worth less or more than the active experience. This issue, which sometimes troubles beginning music therapists, did not concern me. I entirely agree with Bruscia's (1998) explanation of the role of the musical experience in music therapy and the balanced importance he places on both processes: active and receptive (pp. 107–125). The facts were that Nathaniel could hardly use an active musical experience, and I had to support his decision in favor of receptive music therapy:

> It is the client's experience that is at the center of therapy, not the therapist's actions, and because of this, all methodological decisions are based on what the client needs to experience through music (*ibid.,* p. 108).

Conversely, many questions passed through my mind: What should the content of the music be, what emotional material might it elicit, what would the result of a psychodynamic approach be, would it be wise to go into depth, when was it the right moment to delve into Nathaniel's psyche, and when was it appropriate to facilitate comfort, calmness, and the ability to accept death as a continuation of life?

Bright (2002) recommends an examination of our own feelings and attitudes while working with terminal patients. Among other important points, she mentions the possible cultural or religious differences between the patient and the therapist (p. 67). For example: In my country, a religious Jew abides by strict rules and customs, which guide his steps and even his verbal expressions concerning death and mourning. If the therapist is religious and the patient is agnostic, or vice versa, it might arouse difficulties when dealing with such a sensitive stage of life. As therapists, we have to be flexible and work with different populations, but theory doesn't always coincide with emotions and practice. Therefore, we have to double-check our positions, ethics, and honesty. In Nathaniel's case, we came from approximately the same cultural-religious background, so I could remove these obstacles from my mind. Concerning the depth of the therapeutic process, my psychological education, supported by hospital practice, taught me to follow the patient's lead and to consider his ego strength when considering the extent of depth he was ready and able to enter. Accordingly, I decided to allow myself considerable breadth and long-term patience, even though the oncologist had warned that Nathaniel's days were numbered.

As for Nathaniel's illness, my tendency is to go over medical and psychological reports when embarking on therapy with a new patient.

This is due to the notion that we can never know enough and that there are always new developments. Consequently, I again reviewed material concerning lung cancer and psychological approaches for dealing with terminal illness, material dealing with families of terminal patients, and approaches through and the possible contribution of music therapy. In addition, I mobilized my own experience of working with cancer patients. While doing so, it occurred to me that knowledge is in a way a coping mechanism and specifically serves to facilitate a sense of mastery; mastery that is much impaired when facing death. This was also surely true for Nathaniel, whose illness, pain, and fear presented him with a feeling of frustration and loss of mastery. It reinforced his need to be enabled to choose his own musical material and model of music therapy and by that to achieve a certain amount of mastery. Concerning his medical condition, as a music therapist, I certainly did not get a mandate to supply the patient with information.

The Family in a Crisis of Cancer

Blanchard, Albrecht, and Ruckdeschel (1997) discuss the psychological impact of cancer on the patient's family. The research they cite indicates that the spouse becomes as distressed as the cancer patient and that the major concerns are the fear of the cancer's outcome, fear of death (even if the prognosis is good), the loss of mastery, and not being prepared to meet the patient's demands or understand his/her behavior. In addition, the disruption of the family balance and the daily routines requires a new alignment of life.

> Factors influencing family distress include the disease status and treatment; individual variables, such as spouse age, gender, and possibly caregiver optimism; perceived coping efficiency and adequacy of social support; and variables reflecting the functioning of either the patient-spouse dyad or the entire family unit (*ibid.*, p. 193).

Sharon Manne (1998, pp. 188–202) reviewed the literature dealing with cancer in the marital context and examined four questions:

- What is the cancer's psychological impact on the

healthy spouse and on the patient?
- What impact does the cancer have on the quality and communication in the marital relationship?
- How does the social support of the spouse influence the patient's adjustment?
- Does the marital relationship have an impact on the survival of the cancer patient?

Dr. Manne's suggestions place emphasis on the need for a good assessment of the patient's support network, evaluation of the spouse's psychological functioning, the need to provide the spouse with information about the partner's illness and how to care for him, and the importance of encouraging him to participate in a support group.

Nathaniel's wife obtained very good psychological support and was guided in how to deal with the children. After the initial shock, she and Nathaniel began to accept the situation and mobilized their mutual love and friendship for each other and for the children. From time to time crises arose, but each of them did his best to find a solution.

We should consider that Nathaniel's physical alteration from an active man and a successful family supporter could have had some bearing on his psychological condition and trigger deterioration. Nonetheless, Nathaniel did not become bitter or demanding. Rather, he attempted to cling to life and in a way found beauty in his existence: his wife and children, music, poetry, his room and friends.

Children in general are less interested in the details of the illness and more in the future of the ill parent, in the success of the treatment, and in their own future. Still, many times the children mirror the concerns of the parents and feel frustrated when treated in a childish manner by having the truth concealed from them. As Ratenaude (2000) says:

> When they feel they are being left out of important family discussions, even young children experience tension and distrust. … This does not mean that all information and fears about cancer diagnosis or illness should immediately be shared with the child (p. 241).

Indeed, imagination may sometimes be very frightening in comparison to the truth told to the child in a way adequate for his age, developmental stage, and emotional maturity. Nathaniel's three eldest children (14, 16, and 20) received the grave news in a clear, simple way. The youngest (10) was told in a gradual, slower manner, with fewer details concerning the terminal phase of his father's illness. We ought to remember that the youngest son was at his latency stage of development, in which children have both abstract and concrete ideas and concerns about cancer as well as about death. In addition, the schoolteachers of the three younger children obtained information from them regarding their father's illness, and the mother directed them not to be ashamed and not to keep it secret from their friends. In this way, it was anticipated that the family cohesion could survive and that at the same time each child would maintain his/her own activities without guilt feelings. Nathaniel's wife served the children as a good example of honesty with respect to her ability to talk about her difficulties while coping through the help of love and friendship.

Ratenaude (2000) claims that the emotional stress is greatest on a child when the parent of the same sex is ill. In Nathaniel's family, the youngest (10) and the two eldest (16, 20) were boys. The 14-year-old was a girl. She obviously identified with the role of her mother and helped her as much as possible. She also helped her youngest brother with his homework. The eldest was in the army, that is to say, outside the house, and occupied as a combat soldier. When he came home, he demonstrated a "buddy" relationship with his father and through this supported him. The 16-year-old son was a very good student in school and an outstanding basketball player. He no doubt used his busy life to protect himself, as he had more difficulties than the other three in observing his adored father's deterioration. The 14-year-old girl was more interested in visual arts and in nature. She supported her mother and, through that, her father as well. She was a sensitive girl and contributed femininity to the family constellation. The youngest son, a 10-year-old, was by nature a jolly, active boy with many friends, verbal and communicative. I had the feeling that in his distinctive way he was coping with the situation very well. His mother confirmed this idea. Nathaniel's wife told me that she was very worried about her husband's emotional reaction. Generally speaking, he was a tough person, a hero type. However, what had occurred in reality was that his illness had softened his personality and exposed traits of delicacy and sensitivity. She was also worried about the anger and bitterness she felt concerning his many years of smoking, fearing unnecessary conflict. However, she discussed this with him and in a way ventilated her anger. To summarize the family situation: In spite of the disaster that overwhelmed them, they continued to function and managed to preserve the family cohesion in a remarkable way. At this point, I return to the music therapy process.

Music Therapy—Twenty-Nine Sessions

In Nathaniel's case, I will describe and analyze the entire process of music therapy without dividing it into stages as was done in the first chapter.

To emotionally prepare myself for the following music therapy meeting, I did what I always do, a practice learned from Indian medicine men: I improvised freely, both instrumentally and vocally, to find peace of mind and courage.

As promised, I brought a musical composition to the second meeting: a vocal piece sung in the Regina Pacis convent in Holland where my friend Christina served as a nun. This unisono female vocality was recorded by me in the convent and has a pure, silver-sounding character. Nathaniel listened attentively for 10 minutes and requested to hear it again. He did so three times and then asked to keep it for himself. As I had already prepared a copy, I left it for him.

Beyond the music therapist's intentional work and professional thinking, there is always place for intuitive guess and emotional planning. I mention this in relation to the choice of the music. Of course, there was also an element of logic to it: The music was Gregorian, the character was calm and pure, and Nathaniel could not recognize this specific music. Conversely, there were also other possibilities that I did not select. I would like to once again accentuate the power of intuition at certain moments when knowledge is not the only element in life. Perhaps the nearness to death and to a mysterious world, vague and cloudy, compels us to employ intuition in addition to knowledge. After listening to the piece three times, Nathaniel began to talk about his illness, described his fears of death and of leaving his family alone, and said:

> For a short time, I felt peace of mind. This was while I listened to the music. I hope that's what our meetings will generate. Next time, I'll think about my music collection in this respect of

tranquility and peace of mind.

This was a positive example of meeting Nathaniel's therapeutic needs and of the path that began to form itself. It was good that he resumed making his own choices through which he derived a certain amount of mastery and that he was able to talk about his feelings. After 45 minutes, he looked tired but not worried. He closed his eyes and fell asleep.

A month passed by, throughout which Nathaniel chose his own music for mutual listening. When the music stopped, Nathaniel would talk about his feelings or discuss the music. In the meantime, I had met his wife and four children. They seemed to be very interested in what we were doing. I explained briefly but could not invite them into the room, as Nathaniel was opposed to the idea. The three elder children understood what his wife and I explained to them. The youngest son had difficulties; therefore, I requested permission from Nathaniel's wife to invite the children on one occasion to my clinic and give them a separate session. After the parents agreed, they indeed came to my place and we had an active as well as a receptive experience. The eldest son could not come, as he still served in the army, but the other three were very attentive and cooperative. From their musical and verbal reactions, I was under the impression that it was a good decision. They had enough mysteries to deal with concerning their father's condition and death anxiety. By presenting them with an example of music therapy, they could be less anxious. This was specifically true since dealing with musical experiences is to deal with something normal, compared to what transpires during medical treatment. I imagine that it could have been very constructive to continue music therapy with the children, but it was impossible to do so both technically and therapeutically.

Meanwhile, Nathaniel told me that the mutual listening experience was new to him, though he always listened to music at concerts, alone at his work, and at home. Since music therapy is based on interactions between patient and therapist through the experiencing of music, this might explain the change that Nathaniel felt was brought on by the mutual listening and its verbal results.

> Music to which someone listens at home, or plays at home, can
> be extremely moving for the listener or for the performer. This
> does not mean, however, that it necessarily opens up a window

for self-awareness or for a strengthening of personality. In reality, people tend to cling to a professional analytical frame of mind (especially musicians) or to float on clouds of emotional experience … there remains no evidence of a therapeutic process, or the essential linkage which therapy seeks between emotion and intellect. (Sekeles, 1996, p. 43)

Nathaniel was 45 years old, that is to say, at the midpoint stage in his life. Although they have typically established their family and economical security, those who face death at this age have great concerns: They grieve missing out on experiencing new horizons and watching the development of their children and grandchildren and are anxious about how their spouse will manage after their death. Indeed, the social worker guided Nathaniel's wife to reassure him of her independence as well as to demonstrate for him the ability and strength of their children to cope with the situation. I, on the other hand, took the task of reducing the fear and anxiety aroused by his impending death through our specific modality. Again, the religious Jew would have trusted in God and would have prayed for His mercy. This in itself might diminish fear and anxiety. Being an atheist, Nathaniel had other support:

- Listening to music in a protected atmosphere.
- The verbal conversations we had afterward.
- The use of imagination and dreams in a soothing fashion.
- The identification with poetry.

Reading poetry of his choice began to accompany the listening to music. Subsequently discussing the content broadened the scope of therapeutic elaboration.

He asked for poetry in Hebrew and in English. We read the poems of Yehuda Amichai (1983, 1985), who is one of the best 20th-century Israeli poets. Examples of his work translated into English can be read in *Poet Healer* (Spann, 2004), pp. 99, 175, 200. We also read from Emily Dickinson's *Favorite Poems* (1890), Moshe Dor's *Maps of Time* (1978), and Ruth Finer Mintz's (translator and editor) bilingual anthology of *Modern Hebrew Poetry* (1968).

I would like to bring forth one example from this phase:

Nathaniel wanted me to read one of Amichai's poems for him and recalled that he once enjoyed the *Travels of the Last Benjamin of Tudela*. After reading the poem, I asked him which part or idea was the most meaningful for him, and he immediately pointed at:

> ……… *A child who got hurt*
> *or was hit, as he was playing, holds back his tears*
> *and runs to his mother, on a long road of backyards*
> *and alleys and only beside her will he cry.*
> *That's how we, all our lives, hold back*
> *our tears and run on a long road*
> *and the tears are stifled and locked*
> *in our throats. And death is just a good*
> *everlasting cry. Ta-daaaaaa, a long blast of the shofar,*[5]
> *a long cry, a long silence. Sit down. Today.*

(from *The Selected Poetry of Yehuda Amichai*,1996; translation: Stephen Mitchell)

It occurred to me that this poem was filled with symbolism related to Nathaniel's manhood, which didn't allow him to show any weakness or to cry. He might be willing to do so just like a child who finds shelter and the ability to cry in his mother's arms. The cry is locked in the throat, which now symbolized a sensitive area. The notion of breathing a wind instrument to life is well recognized in magical thinking. Here it is being accentuated by the shofar, an ancient, mighty instrument used only in restricted times of danger and holiness. The shofar was also related to his own musical instrument, the French horn. I wondered how conscious and aware Nathaniel was to the emotional content of the poem. When I asked him what he liked in this part of the poem, he answered: "Perhaps the relationship between the child and the adults. Indeed, I feel like a little infant, unable to master my life anymore and not even able to cry out unless I find mother's lap."

When we resumed our conversation, Nathaniel said: "I wish I could blow my horn and again feel the power of my breath." I suggested listening to a composition played by the horn, and he asked if I could improvise on the subject. This was an interesting challenge. With his permission, I decided to use the sound and the rhythmical patterns of the shofar as a motive for development. While playing the piano, I imagined the unique atmosphere of the synagogue on The Day of Atonement with all the people dressed in white, which is the color of pureness, festivity, and the deceased's shroud in Judaism. It helped to attain inspiration.

To improvise for the benefit of another person in therapy differs from free improvisations for your own sake. It requires from one much concentration and to be tuned into the other person's expression, body language, and tone.

This was an example of employing poetry and turning it into music, according to the wishes and needs of the patient. The piano is a very descriptive instrument with a wide range of implementations, from the most subtle content to orchestral strength. In such moments of therapy, one is relieved to have it as a main instrument. Nathaniel listened and for a very long minute did not utter a word. He reacted only in the following session, by shortly commenting: "Last time I received a present from my therapist."

In the last month of therapy and of life, Nathaniel's health deteriorated. He was rushed to the emergency room several times, but his family and he himself wished for him to remain at home. Before what was meant to be our final meeting, he entered a coma, and while lying in bed "listened" to Fauré's Sicilienne. The entire family surrounded his bed. He died an hour later.

At his funeral, there was no music except for the traditional prayers. A month later, at the 30th ceremony, I brought the same Sicilienne played on a tape recorder to the graveyard. In a way, this was the closure of the life-death circle of a man who knew how to gracefully carry himself through life, terminal illness, and death.

Notes

(1) Dr. Jaacov Avni was a prominent Israeli psychiatrist and psychoanalyst. For the past 22 years, he was head of the psychiatric unit at the Hadassah Medical Center, Mount Scopus, in Jerusalem. He was an open-minded person, interested in the art therapies and accommodating in the treatment of mutual patients. Dr. Avni died recently (March 2006) of an illness and left everybody who knew him in deep grief. Dr. Alma Avni passed away in August 2006. She was an internist and had a deep practical and theoretical knowledge of music. Our lifelong friendship

began in 1952; ever after, we accompanied each other in our personal and professional lives. Alma offered me medical knowledge, personal warmth, and love. God bless her soul.

(2) In such cases, the patient is sent to home care with the essential resources: home visits by a physician, nurse, physiotherapist, and occupational therapist. It is subsidized and supervised by the medical insurance fund in which the patient is a member. In Nathaniel's case, he had a visiting physician, a nurse, and a physiotherapist.

(3) Jewish people visit the grave seven days after the funeral, then after 30 days and each year on the date of death. These basic bereavement customs are kept by the religious as well as by most secular Jews. Each of the official visits to the graveyard adds new closure to the death, and its importance is that it is done in the company of family and friends.

(4) Generally speaking, lung cancer does not cause symptoms when it is at its early stages. This is why it might be in an advanced condition when diagnosed. This was the case with Nathaniel: He was a heavy smoker and began coughing when the tumor began to irritate the lining of the airways and caused a shortage of oxygen. In such a case, it is not logical to try a wind instrument even if it is the patient's personal preference.

(5) The shofar is the ritual instrument of the ancient and modern Hebrews. It was a priestly instrument in Biblical times. It was made either of ibex horn, its bell ornamented with gold and played on the New Year, or of ram's horn, with silver ornamentation, used on fast days. Its tone was to be preserved unaltered. The shofar is closely connected to magical symbolism: Its blast destroyed the walls of Jericho, and in the Dead Sea scrolls it is written that during battles, shofar blowers sounded a powerful war cry to instill fear in the hearts of the enemy, while priests blew the six trumpets of killing. In our times, its liturgical use is restricted to the New Year (Rosh Hashanah) and the Day of Atonement (Yom Kippur).

Chapter Four

WHERE HAVE ALL OUR FLOWERS GONE? MUSIC THERAPY WITH A BEREAVED MOTHER AND WIDOW

A CASE ANALYSIS

"I have a hole in my bosom. Never knew of its existence. ... Here in the center of the bosom, a private hell occurred to a woman who just wanted to hold again and again to her love."
(Adi Lelior, 2004, *Till Death Do Us Part,* p. 51)

Dedicated to Anetta and Reuven Shari[1]

INTRODUCTION

Naama, a mother in her forties, had lost her eldest son in a military action behind the "green line." Though this occurred at a time of war, it was not the enemy who killed him, but, as they say in the army, "the fire of our own forces." Throughout the first two years after this accident, Naama continued to function to some extent, though her motivation and efficacy had obviously deteriorated. Then, another blow struck the family, and her husband, following a short period of illness, passed away.

Naama was left with her adolescent son David, who was on the verge of finishing high school. The everyday activities faded away, and her depression was accompanied by self-negligence: From a beautiful, well-dressed, and preserved wife, she turned into an indifferent woman, could not execute her household duties, neglected her son, did not care to eat, and slept very little. After a year in psychotherapy accompanied by antidepressant drugs, she was referred to music therapy, where the work with her continued for three years. Two years after concluding music therapy, she married a widower who brought two daughters to the family nest. Throughout time, all the children left home and Naama's life as part of a couple continued reasonably.

Why was Naama referred to music therapy? The psychiatrist who treated her had claimed that the medication had helped her but that the verbal therapy had not been effective. Conversely, she had told him of her love for music, of the fact that she was moved by music, and of her readiness to try this medium.

Intake and Observation

Naama entered the room, did not look around, collapsed into an armchair, and stayed there. In the short conversation we had, Naama expressed enormous rage concerning the army, her fate, the dead, her losses, herself, and what awaited her in the future. She was very ambivalent and unsure that any therapy might help her. Interestingly enough, she displayed all of this rage while sitting in the armchair in a bent over position, not making hardly any movement and as though spitting the words to get them out of her system. Moreover, she did not raise her voice above mezzo piano. Thus, there was a disparity between the content and the vocal elements of what she said. At a certain moment, this rage content turned into a deep feeling of helplessness, loneliness, and emptiness. Her vocabulary changed, but the musical features remained approximately the same.

The conversation turned to what she expected from music therapy. After a long silence, Naama asked: "Can it energize my body and soul? Can it pour something that will purify my being?" This was a high mountain of expectations: Was it indeed possible? What does music enable, and where are its limitations? How much would Naama cooperate, and how flexible was she? Specializing in the developmental-integrative model, I asked myself what approach and technique I should choose and implement.

Therapeutic Considerations

In the mourning process that Naama had undergone, the past, present, and future had been felt as an empty space, creating a deficiency, deep pain, helplessness, and hopelessness. The fact that Naama could not find a channel for consolatory activity caused me to contemplate her role in the matrimonial relationship: Naama had always had this conflict of developing her professional life versus being a wife and a mother. She chose the second role and became very dependent on her husband and children. After the death of her eldest son and her husband, as I had found with other dependent widows, she could not so easily rebuild a new meaningful life and was not able to care for the remaining youngest son. Generally speaking, the elaboration of personal grief either positively aids in the adaptation of the rest of the family to the bereavement process or influences it negatively. Death in a family causes changes in hierarchy, in resharing duties, in communication, and more. As long as Naama's husband had lived, he had supported her and they had both taken care of the younger child. Though she had not reverted to her former self after her soldier-son was killed, she had nonetheless hung on in a way. When her husband died, the burden became too heavy and she could not prevent her own disintegration.

Avigdor Klingman (1998) says that the death of an offspring is among the most difficult and painful experiences of parents, always perceived and felt as too early and unjustified. A child is an additional part of the parents' egos, specifically in mothers' emotional worlds. In the Israeli society, where many young soldiers are killed during military service, there is also a kind of emotional differentiation between soldiers who had a "heroic death" and soldiers who were killed in an accident. There is a lot of anger (in this case, anger toward those who killed Naama's son). Remarks such as: "nothing to be proud of," "he gave his life to the country for nothing," can be heard from people, including the families of the deceased.[2]

Klingman *(ibid.)* says that according to the general literature on children's deaths, the following factors must be considered: the parents' personality, the age of the child, the cause of death, and the context in which it transpired.

Returning to Naama: As aforementioned, the transformation from a bereaved mother to a bereaved mother and widow led to her deterioration. Moreover, we can add a bereaved brother and son who needed her to function both as a mother and as a father to the constellation. She needed to deal with her son's grief as well as with her own, to organize all the official arrangements, to cope with her loneliness, and to find new meaning in life, as she did not even have a profession or job to get back to. All this was too much for her personality's strength, and she sank into depression, including all the clinical signs.

To confess to the truth, I had no idea as to what would happen in her music therapy sessions, and the fact that verbal psychotherapy had not helped her troubled me a lot. I did not think that music was the answer to all of her problems, and I did not feel omnipotent. With these feelings, I met Naama for the second session.

Tied to a Coffin

Naama entered the room, fell once again into the armchair, and said:

> To tell you the truth. I don't think I can do anything. Most of the time, I feel tied to a coffin, as if I were lying in a grave, unable to breathe. I cannot even concentrate on my youngest son, and I think that he may not need me.

This image of "tied to a coffin," and the idea that her son might not need her, opened a narrow window for work and elaboration through music. I suggested that she transfer this feeling of lying in the coffin, unable to breathe or think, into music. She immediately responded: "No way! But if you can find recorded music that fits this situation, I'll try to listen to it." I screened my "inner library" of art music (which was the category she preferred), in an effort to find the image of "tied to a coffin." After a few minutes, I suggested Lukas Foss's *Echoi* (1961–1963), an aleatoric improvisation for percussion instruments, cello, piano, and cembalo.[3] The composition begins with a very low cluster played in a quick tremolo style. After few minutes, percussion and piano notes are inserted, followed by Baroque themes, which sounds like a fantasy of distortion. I let Naama hear 10 minutes of the beginning, which was intense enough. Naama's reaction was mixed: "This was awesome music. I could hardly stand it, but it perfectly portrayed the horrible stress I feel in the suffocating coffin."

Indeed, my choice of *Echoi* led to a similar feeling of stress and horror, probably due to the realistic sound of the roaring noise. Another reason was the improvisational features of Foss's composition, which could show Naama that this approach exists in the work of well-known artists.

In music therapy, improvisation has a respectful position and acts as one of the main therapeutic languages. It enables to dare even without a preliminary experience. Thus, the expression of feelings is not necessarily accompanied by words. In addition, improvisations act as a chain of associations, freed from the mastery of reason and logic (Sekeles, 2002).

In the third session, we turned back to the theme of being tied to a coffin, and Naama was ready to try to describe it through piano improvisation. Naama used to play the piano when she was young, but she did not spontaneously improvise. I therefore suggested that she choose one note and let me play it on the bass section of the piano. Naama suggested the note of E, and when she felt comfortable with this note, she carefully added her own improvisation. This one note was played in a constant rhythm (basso ostinato), served as a container, and symbolized the narrow space of the coffin. Naama began to play in a stiff, repetitious style and gradually developed the melodic line, the dynamics, and the range of the music. I looked at her face and saw the expression of a child playing with a new toy. This improvisation continued for about 10 minutes and allowed me, at a certain point, to develop the one note into a melodic counterpoint. After finishing, I suggested listening to the recording. Naama consented. She listened intently and afterward commented:

> I have never improvised on the piano, and I never felt free to play in such a way. I reckon that the one note held me in a manner that allowed me to stay in the coffin without being suffocated. At the end, I even stepped out and felt quite good. I would not suspect that I'd be able to describe a feeling like that through music.

Therapeutic Considerations

The ability to "play" with any material; change its shape; remodel it; think about it in an unconventional way; be active, imaginative, and innovative, is the basics of creativity. Musical improvisations enable us to use "divergent thinking," which is characterized by fluent production, multifaceted solutions, spontaneity, and freedom from logical thinking. From our discussions, I learned that Naama was not comfortable without a well-defined framework and that even while cooking she had to use recipes. From this point of view, strengthening her creativity meant providing her with more self-confidence and freedom. Symbolically, improvising on a holding pattern is to cast your own ideas on a sound ground. This is one of the advantages of mutual playing (in this case four-hand piano) and using techniques that do not require professional competencies.

The holding frame is typically a repetitious parameter: rhythmical pattern, harmonic pattern, basso ostinato, an interval, a melodic line, and others. These are phenomena that exist in musical compositions and give the listener a feeling of consistency and confidence. I thought that we might work on broadening Naama's improvisational and emotional horizons by listening to compositions that develop from a narrow space to a wider one and to correspondingly improvise in a similar fashion.

Holding and Containing

Hector Berlioz demonstrates a type of holding frame in the "Pilgrims' Procession," which is the second movement of *Harold in Italy*,[4] by a sounding a repetitious note. Though this note does not resound in an intensive way, it does so very clearly. Naama enjoyed listening to it, noticed the internal counterpoint voices and melodious lines, and in her imagination developed an entire conversation with her late husband. She divulged the content to me after the music was finished. I suggested that she employ a gestalt technique of two chairs and converse again by playing both roles: her husband and herself. In this conversation, Naama gently blamed her husband for deserting her, leaving her alone with her suffering. Though it was said in a very soft voice, I had the feeling that she had partially ventilated her anger. She moved from chair to chair, even changing her voice a bit, and used painful vocabulary to ease her burden, completely ignoring my presence.

This is merely one example of holding parameters in music, which contain the sorrow of the patient and elicit verbal content. Another example was Ravel's *Bolero,* in which the melody is repeated from beginning to end (for 15 to 18 minutes) with changes in texture and dynamics. In addition, there is a repetitious rhythmical pattern typical to the *Bolero* dance.[5] From a therapeutic point of view, this composition contains elements of ecstatic music, specifically the graduate crescendo and varying of the melodic instruments, versus the fixed rhythmical pattern:

There is, however, no accelerando, and thus the musical excitement in ecstatic traditional rituals (Sekeles, 1994), which elicit ecstatic dancing, is far more restricted and diminished in the *Bolero*. Naama reacted to the *Bolero* by deciding to adopt the rhythmical pattern and drummed it on the timpani for nearly 10 minutes. In the beginning, she could not sound the crescendo, but kept the tempo very well. After about three minutes, she added crescendo and acceleration, which are a natural physiological phenomenon. Naama commented on the feeling this kind of drumming gave her: "I felt 'high' as if I was dancing and not playing. Amazing how a simple repetitious melody may have so much strength and the power to energize the listener. It was good."

Returning to the intake meeting, I thought about Naama's response when I asked her what she expected from music therapy: "Can it energize my body and soul? Can it pour something that will purify my being?" Perhaps she had begun to open herself to simple physio-psychological activity and felt the music not only in her head but also in her body and soul. I remembered that I had Ravel's arrangement of the *Bolero* for solo piano. I decided to use it the next session. After a week, Naama arrived and asked to listen to the *Bolero* again. I took the opportunity to suggest that she play the rhythm, just as she had already done, while I played the solo piano. Naama agreed to try this idea. We played it once from beginning to end, and she then suggested: "We can use the same rhythm and improvise a new composition on it." We did this while alternating roles. That is to say, once she improvised and I kept the rhythm, and vice versa. I felt a positive procession of development, and while she was busy playing I observed a mild expression of satisfaction on her face.

Therapeutic Considerations

Both terms, holding and containing, originate in physiology and were adapted to psychology. The fetus is held and contained in his mother's womb, which gives him comfort and confidence. Subsequent to birth, the mother's body and hands carry on this posture and function, which gradually obtains a double meaning: physiological and psychological.

Generally speaking, a holding frame or a frame "inclines to stabilize the therapeutic process and protect the client and the therapist from being overflooded and carried away by situations and actions that they are not yet ready for or unable to cope with" (Rosenheim, 1990, p. 46). In psychotherapy, the frame may be a set therapeutic time and structure, ethical rules, and more, which enable the therapeutic process to develop within it a proper amount of flexibility. In music therapy, we also have specific techniques that supply a holding frame and at the same time allow freedom for improvisations. This is a duality, typical to music as an art form, which is present in almost all musical categories. With each patient, the holding frame may be a different structural element: rhythm, melody, harmony, etc. We therefore need to find the most effective element and work with it while internalizing, conversing, reflecting, augmenting, clarifying, and more.

Naama was able to listen in a sensitive way, gradually represented actual life events through music, and used it to suit her particular needs. An example of this is the conversation she held with her husband in which she ventilated her anger toward him for the very first time.

An additional sign of progress was her growing ability to improvise freely and to feel good about it. Besides its other advantages, playing freely may sometimes impart on the improviser an elated feeling of happiness. Indeed, this linguistic connection in English (and in some other languages) between "playing" and "playing" a music instrument has great meaning. A smiling expression, which was uncommon for her, gradually began to appear on Naama's face. A tiny light at the end of the obscure tunnel through which we walked together seemed to appear.

It is significant to again emphasize that musical interaction in music therapy is perceived as analogous to life itself. I felt that Naama had gradually learned through the musical interaction that experiencing death, as difficult as it might be, was also a universal experience of life. One might develop personal meaning concerning life and death even when it seems as though life has lost its value and that we are imprisoned with the dead in their graves.

Naama also began to understand that the worn-out term "coping" contains subterms such as adaptation, indulgence, giving, and the need to change life molds in order to establish psychological and spiritual independence.

Mother-Son Music Therapy

At a certain therapeutic moment, Naama brought her relationship with David, her youngest son, to therapy. She conveyed it verbally and described her guilt feelings and the minimal care she was able to provide him: "I expect him to understand my condition and most of the time to forget his young age and own needs." During this conversation, we discussed a possibility she suggested, of mother-son music therapy. At that moment, it seemed a good suggestion and we decided to try it. This therapeutic process lasted till the conclusion of therapy and exposed many layers of pain and anger on both sides. By this time, David had already finished high school and had obtained a deferment from the army for the purpose of premilitary studies. I would like to present a few examples from this period and demonstrate the role music therapy played in this voyage:

TOGETHERNESS: David entered the music therapy room with his mother, who informed him that he was allowed to freely explore the musical instruments. From this point on, I observed the two and the musical and extramusical interaction that transpired between them. David had no problem trying the drums, the bells, the wind, the string and self-made instruments. At first, Naama just watched him without any interference, but at a certain moment she gently joined him. He was playing the lyre, and she added Japanese bells. In a moment of intermission, I requested permission to record their mutual creation, and they agreed. Naama and her son David spent the entire hour improvising without a directing subject, rules, or instructions. I did not see any reason to join in or to interfere.

RELISTENING: Next session, I suggested listening to some parts of their improvisations from the previous week. They agreed and did so very carefully. I noted that David had good concentration qualities in addition to his creative freedom. Following the listening exposition, he declared: "It is fun but we have to practice a lot if we want to be together." His mother responded: "Yes, you are right, but here in music therapy we are not provided with corrective instruction. We have to find our way together."

IMPROVISATIONS: David and Naama improvised with musical instruments for an entire month. During this period, they showed no inclination to describe a situation, a feeling, a figure, etc. Neither did they use their voice musically, although it is the closest element to speech. On the other hand, the improvisations became more and more developed and clearly structured, with dynamical changes; at times, they were even divided into semichapters. It was amazing to see how a musical interaction could develop without planning or words. My role at that time was to let them be and work together in a way and through a modality foreign to them, to allow them to experience mutuality detached from everyday life. They occasionally asked for my help, mainly on technical matters, or requested that I replay their improvisations.

CLINICAL IMPROVISATIONS: After about a month, Naama told David that in her music therapy sessions she also experienced conversing, representing, describing her feelings, and more through improvisations. Coming from Naama (and not from the therapist), this was undoubtedly a turning point. Where would it lead them? Us? David suggested: "I like jazz and rock, you certainly prefer your classical music. Perhaps we can first represent ourselves through precomposed music?" Naama accepted this idea, and for several sessions they listened to their musical choices, after which they developed interesting conversations. They gradually began to request my involvement, and we entered a phase in which Naama and I improvised together on the piano and David and I played his material. I would play the piano and he the drums and other percussion instruments. This process did not bring David any closer to his mother's preferences, but drew Naama closer to her son's music and she joined in his playing, showing new interest.

WHERE HAS ALL OUR ANGER GONE? The final segment of music therapy with Naama and David was the longest and dealt with bitter feelings, anger, grieving for the deceased brother and father, and confronting mother-son emotions and each other, as difficult and painful as this was. The musical work they had invested in so far was very efficient in building a mutual relationship of confidence, and thus the ground was ripe for embarking on this new level. Once again, as in previous cases I have analyzed, patience was the key ingredient. In his chapter on dealing with anger and guilt, Parkes (1972) emphasizes the notion that "until the reality of the loss has been fully accepted, the greatest danger is the danger of the loss itself. The bereaved person still feels that the dead person is recoverable, and anything that brings home the loss is reacted to as a major threat. Relatives and friends who try to induce a widow to stop grieving before she is ready to do so, or even those who indicate that grief will pass, are surprised at her indignant response. It is as if they are obstructing the search for the one who is lost" (p. 80).

I felt that since her mutual therapy with her son, Naama was on the verge of a better insight due to her revitalizing experiences and elicited more energy and acceptance. Developing insight mostly requires interference and guidance on the part of the therapist. With the therapist's encouragement, Naama and David began to learn to express those parts in each of them that were silenced and distorted for a long time. Confrontation was necessary in order to begin an intra and inter dialogue. This therapeutic process was technically prompted through both musical and verbal conversations. At that point, they also began to employ musical vocality, which seemed uncomfortable to each of them. David was the first to realize that singing can increase the emotional possibilities of the vocal expression, as it holds many possibilities less exploited in speech: accentuation through many repetitions of one motive, rich emotional expression by using a wide vocal range, and more. Despite the embarrassment, the vocal dialogues they began to develop deepened the process of peeling away their protective layers of armor. David expressed his anger at his mother for investing all of her emotions in his deceased brother and later in his deceased father, though before her stood her surviving son, who was faced with overcoming a difficult period of matriculations, grieving, and mourning: "You barely asked me about my examinations, not to mention my feelings. You hardly ever cooked; you neglected every motherly function and walked around the house like a zombie." Naama's response was a cry that she was unable to end. A week later, she collected herself and said to David: "You were always the strongest in the family, stronger than your brother and father and surely stronger than me. I had the feeling that you did not need me, but it was also very convenient for me to think so, as I had no energy to invest or share." At moments such as these, the therapist's role was to facilitate a reassuring atmosphere, relating that the world continues to exist and that we do not come apart or dissolve when we discharge our conflicts with our beloved ones.

The second step was to discuss the son-brother and husband-father deaths. It appeared that David had experienced many conflicts with his elder brother, but felt that he was not allowed to desecrate his mother's memories or the memory of the dead. He missed his brother in an "unfinished business" dynamic and desperately needed to elaborate on the subject. I initially suggested working on it by representing the family members through musical instruments and voice. He first worked alone and later with his mother. Since his relationship with his father was very good, it was easier for David to express the immense anger toward his brother. I must admit that these recordings are among the most touching pieces I ever experienced in therapy. The more David and Naama externalized their emotions, the better they began to feel. Concerning Naama, her everyday functioning became nearly regularized, and the termination of music therapy painted the horizon.

MUSIC AND POETRY. During this stage, singing became part of the sessions, including Israeli songs accompanied by the therapist. This soon led to the writing of poetry and sometimes to the composing of music to it. The latter process had many faces: Sometimes each of them wrote a poem with regard to him/herself without or with music; other times, Naama wrote a poem and David composed the melody or vise versa. Their style was very different, but the mutual feature was the discovery of a personal talent and artistic satisfaction. I would like to present the translation of Naama's final poem, to which David composed accompanying music. We must of course take note of the fact that the translation from Hebrew to English changes the musical intonation of the text itself, but I tried to stay true to the original meaning:

> *Death bit crudely at my heart*
> *Left me in my grave dead-alive*
> *Bless God for opening my eyes*
> *to beauty and to the sounds of music*
> *Bless God for a compassionate last moment*
> *of salvation*
> *Bless God for purifying my heart*
> *to feel the pain and to accept the joy.*

Bless my life-friend for leaving me the sweet memories
of the dead and the alive.

SUMMARY

Sometimes we title a therapeutic process as though it were a musical form, such as a sonata, rondo, etc. In Naama's case, I received the impression of a "fantasia form" due to the fact that we walked through endless curves, turned in all directions, experienced regression and gradually felt new drops of life and insight. From the stage that Naama understood the urgent need to work through her relationship with her son David, the road turned from a stony-thorny path to a paved one. Music improvisation and receptive music therapy from time to time were the modalities that paved this road and the intra and inter mother-son relationship. Through this work, the relationship with the deceased became clearer and Naama was able to open her heart to grief and bereavement without fearing the disintegration of her own personality.

As mentioned in the introduction, Naama re-married two years after concluding music therapy. During this period, she dedicated time to the piano, which she had ceased to play upon concluding elementary school. She resumed lessons and spent time improvising. Her son, David, completed his studies and his army service (unharmed).

It is essential to mention that the process of music therapy was concluded with the consent of both patients and therapist. It seemed like the right moment, though as Rosenheim (1990) says: "Sharpening the coping tools does not guarantee a 'security certificate' for resisting future pressures…" (p. 20☐). It does however increase the likelihood of coping better, with reduced anxiety, when encountering a new obstacle in life.

Notes

(1) Anetta (1903-1978) and Reuven Shari (1902-1989) were born in Russia. They were both among the compelled "numerous clauses" in their high school, which they finished "com laude" at a very young age. Reuven studied further and became a young lawyer; Anetta studied dentistry and played the piano. The anti-Jewish programs, which had not

ceased since 1821 (1859, 1881–1884, 1903–1906, 1917), left hundreds of thousands of Jews dead. In the 1917 Russian Revolution alone 250,000 civilian Jews died, many were wounded, and 2 million emigrated, mainly to America and partly to Israel (Rubinstein, Chon-Sherbok, Edelhei, & Rubinstein, 2002). Anetta and Reuven were young parents of their first baby daughter when they immigrated/escaped in 1925 to Israel. In the new country, they had to stop their intellectual activities and work like other pioneers in agriculture, in paving roads, in building Israel. In the forties, Reuven turned back to law and contributed intensively to the public life of Israel. In 1948, he became a member of the Knesset, head of civil service, and more. By decision, Anetta took responsibility for the home and the raising of her three daughters. This chapter is dedicated to my beloved parents, Anetta and Reuven Shari, who taught us the meaning of family, of work, of art, and of a motherland.

(2) Comparing the grieving of mothers to that of fathers: Mothers display their grief more openly than fathers. There is less research concerning the grief of fathers, but in Israel they take on the role of the strong family member. It is important to remember that most of them served in the Israeli army and had experienced death related situations as soldiers. They tend to be in more of a position of denial, their mourning period is shorter than that of the mothers, and they go back to work as soon as possible. On the other hand, there were several cases in Israel in which fathers (including some high officers) committed suicide at the grave of their soldier-son.

(3) Lukas Foss is a German-born composer who immigrated to America. In 1956, he began to work on improvisations with his students at UCLA, which led him to form the Improvisation Chamber Ensemble. They did a lot of aleatoric work and contributed important new concepts to art music.

(4) *Harold in Italy* was ordered by Paganini in 1834 as a viola concerto for his Stradivarius instrument. Berlioz remained one year in Italy and adored the landscape. The composition, ready in 1835, was influenced by these images. Paganini was not satisfied with the results, as the viola role in this composition did not show enough prominence. Still, it presents a

special intrinsic relationship between the orchestra and the viola.

(5) Maurice Ravel (1875–1937) composed the *Bolero* for ballet based on the traditional Spanish form. It consists of a repetitive melody, a counter-melody, gradual crescendo, a large orchestra, and changes in instrumental texture with condensation towards the end. Therapeutically speaking, it has a stable frame, which includes the rhythmical pattern and the melodic line. Changes of orchestration and volume occur on this foundation. Based on my clinical experience, most patients feel good with this composition. There are those who need repetitions and others who can perceive the gradual changes and enjoy them. Some patients like to express this music in movement or graphically, imitate the rhythm, and more. While working with dance therapists, I instructed them to translate the *Bolero*'s musical components into movement. The videotaped results were very interesting, as we could observe unusual interactions between limbs, interesting choices of body parts to express the rhythm, difficulties in keeping the tempo solid while the dynamics changed, etc.

Chapter Five

THE RELATION BETWEEN ART MUSIC, DEATH, AND GRIEF

"You are anxious to know the secret of death, but how shall you find it
unless you seek it in the heart of life?"
(Gibran Khalil Gibran, 1923, *The Prophet,* on death)

Dedicated to Prof. Kalman Benyamini[1]

The title of this chapter immediately overwhelmed me with an abundance of material, since death as well as love is represented in many compositions, categories, and musical cultures.

It is possible to examine the subject chronologically or categorically such as through religious music, ethnic music, art music, etc. My personal choice fell on art music. In music therapy, we use art music as needed for therapeutic considerations, such as to facilitate relaxation or excitation, to elicit and guide movement, to empathize with a certain feeling, to guide imagination and fantasy, to assist the elaboration of a process, to encourage verbal conversation, and more.

After considering the issue, I decided to focus mainly in this chapter on a few musical examples, primarily of the 19th and 20th centuries, that are rich in descriptive titles and have a natural association with other artistic modalities. Throughout these centuries, the content was often expressed verbally by the composer for either personal reasons or the general tendency of the period to unite music, poetry, theater, and literature.

During the search for compositions dealing with death and mourning, I went over a lot of known and less known material and found that although the music was in certain cases clouded with heavy or dark colors, it was also possible to derive from it comfort and peace of mind. Leonard Meyer (1956) argues that

In Western culture, for example, grief is communicated by a

special type of behavior: physical gestures and motor behavior tend to minimal; facial expression reflects the cultural picture of sorrow; the range of vocal expression is confined and often sporadic; weeping customary; and dress too serves as a behavioral sign. It is this special, sanctioned picture of grief which is communicated in Western music (pp. 266–267).

Although Meyer suggested that the same phenomena could be observed through music, when we examine music dealing with death and mourning, even in one specific culture and in a particular era, we find varied expressions parallel to the different stages of grief. We can therefore speak of pieces that deny death, such as the fourth song in Gustave Mahler's *Songs on the Death of Children (Kindertotenlieder)*, in which the title already transmits a feeling of denial ("Often I think that they have only stepped out") or pieces in which the grief is transferred into a warlike, aggressive anger, as in some parts of Leonard Bernstein's *Halil*, or when it is dark, solemn, and depressive, as in the second movement of Anton Bruckner's Seventh Symphony; or when it is tender and reconcilable with death, as in the Sicilienne, part 3, in Gabriel Fauré's Suite, op. 80, *Pelléas and Mélisande*. We can learn of Fauré's attitude toward death from a letter he wrote in 1902 to a friend (in Nectoux, 1984): He saw death as a joyful deliverance, an aspiration toward a happiness beyond the grave, rather than a painful experience.

It is easier to talk about the transmission of emotion when text is involved. However, what are the musical factors and parameters that depict a specific feeling to the listener? Can music express an emotion? If it can, is it an international phenomena or just the way that a certain composer conceptualizes human feelings? Or is it the projection of the listener that elicits a certain interpretation and identification? These questions and more are present and important in music therapy as well as in the philosophy of music and art. In regard to this, Suzanne Langer (1982) states:

Music is not self-expression, but formulation and representation of emotions, moods, mental tensions, and resolutions—a "logical picture" of sentient, responsive life, a source of insight, not a plea for sympathy. Feelings revealed in music are essentially not "the passion, a love or longing of such-and-such an individual," inviting us to put ourselves in that individual's place, but are presented directly to our understanding, that we may grasp, realize, comprehend these feelings, without pretending to have them or imputing them to anyone else (p. 222).

Let us take, for example, Frederic Chopin's "Funeral March" (the third movement of the Second Piano Sonata in B flat minor, 1837). The "Funeral March" became so famous that it is often used as an iconic representation of grief. Indeed, it was written as a funeral piece and Chopin himself entitled it, but nevertheless, it was not inspired by any specific personal death and mourning. Generally speaking, the structure of this sonata (grave, scherzo, funeral march, presto) already guarantees an architectural dynamic, which accentuates this third movement. The "Funeral March" was composed in an A-B-A form. Section A includes a melody, using full chords; a basso obstinate, which walks consistently and heavily in the lower part of the piano; and an intense crescendo. In a therapeutic language, we might say that the bass supplies a "holding frame," while its contrast with the chords and the dynamical changes gives the whole part a dramatic touch. In the B section (D flat major), the right hand plays a lyrical melody while the left hand moves in a soft arpeggio. The tempo is mild, the general character is more contemplating than dark, and there is only a mild crescendo. Thus, this part maintains a calm-soft, cradlelike atmosphere in contrast to the dramatic dynamics of the A section. The second A (back to B flat minor) emerges from the B, develops to fortissimo, and closes quietly. More than once, I have heard patients say that the B section of the "Funeral March" gave them a sense of consolation. Edi, who lost his wife in a terror attack, requested to listen to the composition and described the B section in these words: "as if the sky brightened and a few sun rays emerged through the dark heaven." In other words, listeners may identify with the representation of an emotion, transferred by the composer, as Langer formulated it. This ability to identify is very important both in everyday life and, obviously, in music therapy.

Returning to Chopin's example, in *The Critic as an Artist,* Oscar Wilde (1890) wrote:

> After playing Chopin, I feel as if I had been weeping over sins that I had never committed, and mourning over tragedies that

were not my own. Music always seems to me to produce that effect. It creates for one a past of which one has been ignorant and fills one with a sense of sorrows that have been hidden from one's tears (p. 6).

Jeremy Siepmann (1995) quotes Arthur Rubinstein's words in the biography he wrote about Chopin:

> It does not tell stories or paint pictures. It is expressive and personal, but still a pure art. Even in this abstract atomic age, where emotion is not fashionable, Chopin endures. His music is the universal language of human communication. When I play Chopin, I know I speak directly to the hearts of people (p. 5).

Chopin was not describing a real death event, but we can assume that he transmitted his personal experiences through his music: the exile from his beloved Poland at the age of 20, tuberculosis, disappointments in romance, and more, till his death at the age of 38. After his death, Hector Berlioz commented that Chopin was dying all his life. Is it possible to hear a direct expression of that in his music? Is it important to have an explicit expression in order to have an emotional communication between the music and the listener? Does the way in which the composer elaborates on an emotion through the compositional process draw us closer or further away from emotional identification? Is it possible that the artistic elaboration alone enables the listener to identify with the emotion although "the blood is not spread all over the walls," but rather symbolizes the grief and misery?

Similarly, quiet-nostalgic Israeli songs heard on the radio on national remembrance days help most people identify with the grief, although the music does not portray a knife stabbing at our throats (a subject dealt with in the second chapter of this book).

Throughout the years, I tended to note people's reactions (patients and nonpatients, musicians and nonmusicians) to different art music compositions. I discovered that most of them perceive the low register and the slow tempo as a symbol of "the earth's kingdom," while melodic music played by a clear wind or string instrument or voice in its higher register as "the kingdom of heaven." These concepts of earth and sky also symbolize subjects such as death and life, imprisonment and freedom, hell and paradise. The same phenomena can be observed in therapy through patients' choices of musical instruments, which may represent issues such as life and death. Indeed, in many compositions, the underworld of the afterlife is depicted by low musical instruments or in any case by a deeper range, slow tempo, etc. The second movement of Bruckner's Seventh Symphony serves as such an example, as does the third act of Monteverdi's *L'Orfeo,*[2] in which Charon, the guard of the Hades, has a bass voice, and the world of the dead is illustrated through low brass instruments. On the other hand, the heavenly world is generally represented by a flute, voice, harp, lyre, and so on, mostly in an allegro or milder tempo: In his Sicilienne,[3] which is the third movement of Fauré's Suite, op. 80, *Pelléas and Mélisande,* a soft melody is played by the flute, accompanied by the harp and the orchestra in a sweet delicacy, though it depicts death. This is also the case in "Pie Jesu" from Fauré's Requiem, op. 48, for soprano and orchestra: "Gentle Lord Jesus, grant them rest; grant them eternal rest," as well as in the third movement, "Silence and Devotion," of Ernest Bloch's *Sacred Service.*[4]

This is of course a generalization of the subject, and many times the combination of both conveys to the listener a feeling of a tragedy or a conflict that emerges from the depths of the soul. Penderecki's "Dies Irae" *(Auschwitz Oratorium),* which combines low instrumentation with a high soprano, is a good example of this. In this case, the high-pitched singer is screaming as if desperately splitting the sky. Indeed, one of the techniques to build drama in music is to accentuate contradiction or dualism (see also Sekeles, 1996, chapter 2: "Psychoacoustic Qualities of Musical Parameters and their Therapeutic Relevance," pp. 34–41).

Hector Berlioz (1841) composed the music to Théophile Gautier's *Summer Nights (Les Nuits d'Été).* These six songs (Gautier originally entitled the cycle *The Comedy of Death*) were meant to be performed by a baritone or mezzo-soprano and a piano. Later on, Berlioz arranged it for mezzo-soprano and orchestra (final version, 1856).

Summer Nights describes the death of a beloved girl and gradually develops the feeling of disaster: The first song, "Street Song" (Villanelle), portrays the two lovers in nature. The mezzo-soprano sings a fluent melody while the orchestra plays in nonlegato rhythm. This dualism imparts a feeling of wishful thinking and ominous feeling in this pastoral scene. The second song, "The Specter of the Rose," reminds us of the dead girl. Death is felt in the sad melody, which emerges after quite a long introduction. In the third song, "On the Lagoons" (Lamento), the lover laments his beloved, which is a step toward grief and the absence. In this song, Berlioz shifts to a minor key and the trombones and wind instruments express the pain in their low voice. From within the quiet grief develops a cry uttered in a high key, descending chromaticism, and a crescendo. This cry is repeated several times, and the dualism here is between the melancholic melody and the powerful high cry. The fourth song, "Absence," accentuates the feeling of yearning. The song returns to a major key as the lover begs his beloved to come back. The fifth song, "In the Cemetery" (Lamento), describes the cemetery in the moonlight, and the sixth one, "The Unknown Island" (Barcarolle), gives the illusion of a happy, soft ending, but it in fact conceals frustration and pain when the final question of the lover fades into a silence. The relationship between the singing voice and the orchestra creates a very dramatic atmosphere.

The title of the cycle is Berlioz's own, and it may be considered the first unequivocal contribution to the French repertoire of art song. Personally, Berlioz was experiencing a very difficult period in relation to his marriage at that time, and we can assume that he probably transmitted his suffering, consciously or unconsciously, into his music. Later on, in 1867 he lost his beloved son, his health condition deteriorated, and in March 1869 he died in Paris. In his diary, Berlioz admits that:

- He had melancholic tendencies from an early compositional age: "My youthful compositions all bore the stamp of profound melancholy. Almost all my melodies were in minor keys, and although I knew this to be a defect, I could not help it" (Berlioz *Mémoires,* 1966, chapter 14, p. 14).
- He had an urge to interlace emotional events in his musical compositions: "When I began, in 1829, to write my *Symphonie Fantastique,* the melody [which he wrote in his young compositional days after a discouraging love story] came back to me, and, as it seemed to express the overwhelming grief of a young heart in the pangs of hopeless passion, I welcomed it. It is the Air for the first violins at the opening of the Reveries, Passions; I put it in just as it was" (*ibid.,* p. 15).

It may be a presentation of an emotion, but it is important to note that the composer is aware of the transformation of his own feeling into a musical creation. As music therapists, this is one of the objectives we strive to facilitate in our patients, mostly through improvisations. In therapy, expressing feelings through music is not a scientific action of exactness but rather a heart-to-heart nonverbal experience.

I chose the last song of the cycle as an example to examine the impressions of varied listeners: about 35 adults (clients and students) listened to the *Summer Nights* cycle during the last five years. Only 10 people understood the French text and related to it; the rest said that what they felt had been transmitted purely through the music.

The Unknown Isle (poem no. 6)

Tell me, pretty young maid,
where would you like to go?
the sail unfurls like a wing,
the breeze is about to blow.

The oar is of ivory,
the flag of watered silk.
the rudder of fine gold;
for ballast I have an orange,

for sail an angel's wing,
for ship's boy a seraph.

Tell me, pretty young maid, etc.
Would it be to the Baltic,
or to the Pacific?
or to the isle of Java?
or else would it be to Norway,
to pluck the snow flower
or the flower of Angsoka?

Tell me; tell me, pretty young maid,
Tell me where would you like to go?

Take me, said the pretty young maid
to the faithful shore
where love endures forever.

The shore, my dear, is barely known
in the realm of love
Where would you like to go?
The breeze is about to blow.

(English translation: Tess Knighton. From the booklet of the EMI Recording of Jose Van Dam and Jean-Philippe Collard, CDC 7 492882)

The impressions described from the sixth song were as follows: most people thought that it was a love song, some said that it described the desperation of a loving lady (probably because of the mezzo-soprano). Two patients suffering from depression felt that the lady was at the point of committing suicide and that in her singing she was expressing a desperate cry for help. One of the schizoid patients said: "I do not understand the language, but this woman is lamenting somebody. I think she lost her children."

It is always amazing how music, which is a very abstract art, may transmit or describe similar feelings to different people, either healthy or sick. In this case, the text (even for the few who understood the language) does not speak directly of feelings but rather used metaphorical description and suggestions of "places to go." However, the listeners did not receive any guidance as to the content from the therapist. Moreover, most of them did not like the music and felt overwhelmed by the singing. Those who empathized with the music said that it was stronger than words and therefore they did not mind not understanding the language.

Jean Paul (Johann Paul Friedrich Richter), the Bavarian author (1763–1825), said of the romantic music of the era:

> O Music! Thou who bringest past and future so near our wounds with their flying flames! O Music! Reverberation from a distant world of harmony! Sigh of the angel within us! When the word is speechless, and the embrace, and the eye, and the tear; when our dumb hearts lie lonely behind the ironwork of our breasts — then it is Thou alone through whom they call to one another in their dungeons sighs. (In Strunk, 1950, pp. 850–851)

It appears as if the drama which takes place in the second movement of Anton Bruckner's Seventh Symphony in C sharp minor transmits this feeling. While writing this part, Bruckner said that he had a premonition of disaster concerning the impending death of Richard Wagner, a composer he admired. Under the influence of this frame of mind, he wrote the second movement, dedicated to Wagner. Indeed, after a while Wagner died and Bruckner added a lamentation coda. The entire symphony was dedicated to King Ludwig II from Bavaria, who was Wagner's patron. In relation to this, the musicologist John Naglee Burk (1939) commented:

> It is a wonder that Bruckner, the neglected, poor, humiliated schoolmaster, grotesque in his appearance, a farmer in his manners and speech, experienced the day of reckoning and spoke musically as in the tongue of the angles (p. 101).

Concerning what has already been said regarding the sentiment that low-pitched musical instruments convey, we ought to take note of the orchestration of the string instruments combined with two tenor tubas, two bass tubas, and one contrabass tuba. It is quite obvious that there is a feeling of "the day of reckoning."

Friedrich Rucket (1788–1866), the German poet, wrote five poems titled *Songs on the Death of Children (Kindertotenlieder)*. He wrote it after losing his two daughters to a malady.[5] Gustave Mahler received this cycle in 1901 while he was already 41, busy with his Fifth Symphony, and set two of the poems to music. A year after he married Alma-Maria and in 1904 while composing his Sixth Symphony, he decided to focus on the additional four poems. At that time, he had two little daughters of his own, and one version claims that Alma-Maria objected to the work on the poems, fearing the evil eye. Nonetheless, Mahler insisted, and the conflict between them, among other problems, cast a shadow on their relationship. In 1907, his daughter Maria-Ana died. Mahler never overcame his grief after the death of his daughter. It may be that the death of his daughter awoke bitter memories from his own tragic childhood when he lost, among others, his beloved brother Ernst. In the concluding segment of his Ninth Symphony, there is a citation from the second poem: "Now I see well why with such dark flames your eyes sparkled so often," a line that musically contributes to a climax. Ovidius (43 B.C.–A.D. 18) said that songs do not guarantee immunization against death. No doubt Alma-Maria Mahler would agree with him.

The first song speaks of the fact that life goes on despite the occurrence of a personal tragedy: "Misfortune came to me alone, but the sun shines on everyone." The focus of the second song is on the deep pain of loss dressed in a mystic light: "What now are beloved eyes to you will be only stars in the night to come." The third song longs for the fulfillment of a fantasy: "When your dear mother comes on in shimmering candlelight, it is for me as though still you came in with her as you used to do." The fourth song is as aforementioned, an example of denial: "We will meet again on the hills in the sunshine!" The fifth song accepts death by first describing the horrors outside: "In such a weather, in such a tempest, I'd never sent the children out!" and then in the last stanza the poet-father pacifies himself: "They rest as if in their mother's house, where no storm can frighten them, and God's hand shelter them."

I have chosen to examine the fourth poem (set to music in 1902):

Often I think that they have merely gone out
soon they will be coming home again!

The day is bright—Oh, never fear!
They have only gone for a long walk.

Yes: they have merely gone out
And soon they will be coming home again!

Oh, never fear! The day is bright!
They have just taken a walk to the hills over there.

They've merely gone ahead of us
And will not be coming home again!
We will meet again on the hills,
In the sunshine! The day is bright
on those hills over there.

(English translation: Sony Music Entertainment, 1991)

It is interesting to follow the relationship between the text and melody: The orchestra, which includes woodwind instruments, horn, harp, and strings, begins with a flowing melody, hinting at the theme of the solo section and preparing its entry. The presence of chromaticism creates an ambiguous mood of hope blended with sadness. There is a perfect continuity between the solo and the orchestra, and the orchestration supports the textual content: descending in chromaticism in sections where anxiety is expressed and ascending in places where hope is expressed. At the closure of the first section appear a crescendo and a widening of diapason where the words are: "Oh, never fear!" The third section accentuates the fact that they will never return home with an additional dramatic crescendo, which takes us from pp to ff. The three final bars finish on pp/ppp, creating a somewhat delusional sadness. This song is very dramatic in character due to the musical components: a wide range of voice-melody and of volume and rich harmonization. All these follow, support, and describe the tragic poem.

In the 1973 war, Yadin Tannenbaum, an 18-year-old Israeli soldier, was killed. Yadin was a gifted flautist. Leonard Bernstein heard his playing and, though he had never met him before, decided to write a composition "in memory of Yadin's soul and his soldier-brothers." This composition is titled *Halil,* meaning a flute in Hebrew. It should also be mentioned that two other words stem from the same grammatical origin: void = halal (also hollow = halal) and dead in battle. The blowing of a flute is an ancient symbol of life (breath) and the hollow within the instrument is spelled exactly like the word halal (dead or fallen in battle).

Bernstein clearly stated that he uses music to create and symbolize the struggle between life and death and the aspiration for love, hope, and peace. Indeed, he uses (not unusual in his compositions) tonality juxtaposed with atonality, drums, cymbals, tremolo, and powerful dynamics to approach the darkness of earth and the flute as a symbol of spirituality and eternity.

The composition begins with a full, threatening orchestral reverberation from which the crying voice of the flute is elicited. The flute proceeds with a low-pitched melody while the orchestra remains in the background. In the relationship between the flute and the strings, even when the flute is playing a jerky, pseudo-jolly melody, the orchestra continues to remind us of the tragedy. Toward the end, there is a sort of reserved conclusion of the combat, where the flute evaporates in a long-lonely sound.

One of my patients who was going through a profound process of mourning for his mother commented after listening to *Halil:* "The storm that Bernstein evokes connects me to the deepest grave I know, the grave which dwells inside me, and in this part where the flute converses with the strings, I feel that my stomach is sending out thin threads of secrets" (J., 1990).

SUMMARY

In choosing a few examples of art music related to death and grief, I have attempted to demonstrate that there are compositions that might be used in life and in therapy to facilitate an expression of a feeling that may aid the listener. In some of the case analyses, I attempted to show in detail how this kind of receptive music therapy might occur. As a result of many years of observations within music therapy sessions, I tend to believe that it is the artistic elaboration of the feelings of grief that make it possible for listeners to identify and ventilate some of their own emotional burden. On the other hand, we have the clinical improvisations used in active music therapy as a main language, through which patients express their grief, not necessarily in an artistic way, but rather in the spontaneous style of a layman. Still, we should remember that music therapy as a profession would not exist without music as such. Thus, we must learn in depth of its potential possibilities in, as, and for therapy.

I rarely used compositions that were intentionally created for burial ceremonies and have a well-known form, such as the *Requiem Mass*[6] or operas that are related to death and mourning scenes.[7] There ought to be a separate chapter to deal with death and mourning in relation to integrative artistic forms such as opera[8] or the requiem mass.

Every music therapist can select his own collection of art music examples. In a way, the compositions we choose or sometimes use in receptive music therapy partly reflect our own personality. This specifically occurs with patients who do not want or are unable to make decisions. It actually happens both in receptive and in active music therapy. In most cases, we encourage the patients to make choices, but if this does not happen we must have patience and be aware of the process without pushing the client. With some patients, the ability to initiate will never come: Amos, a severely brain-damaged patient as the result of a severe accident, used to play the violin. In addition to his quadriplegia, he gradually lost his ability to speak. However, while he could still converse, he said to me: "When I listen to this Beethoven's concerto, I imagine that I am the violinist and this fantasy allows me a moment of strength, though it is merely a fantasy. I am happy that my ears were not damaged and that while listening to music they can take the role of my hands."

Notes

(1) Prof. Kalman Benyamini taught clinical psychology at The Hebrew University of Jerusalem. He contributed to the development of School Psychological Services in Israel and helped establish the Community Stress Preventive Center in Kiriat Shmona (Galilee). He was a researcher, a writer, and an editor *(Megamot Quarterly)*. I dedicate this chapter to Prof. Kalman Benyamini, my brother-in-law, a wise scholar, and a lover of music until his last day (1995).

(2) *L'Orfeo. Favola in Musica* (1607) is a most important early opera of the 17th century. Monteverdi designed the role of the musical instruments according to the content of the text. There is a definite

analogy between the dramatic development and the vocal/instrumental orchestration. Tragic events are depicted through low-register choruses, wind instruments, and a continuo regal. Thus, the descending of Orfeo to the underworld is really colored in dark tints.

(3) The Sicilienne was originally composed for the cello (1893), and later on Fauré rescored it as part of the suite *Pelléas and Mélisande.* There is a definite difference in atmosphere between the performance of the cello and that of the flute.

(4) Four voices coro a cappella, in F sharp minor; dynamics range between pp-p except for the highest, and only F note in this segment is performed with mf on the word "Redeemer." The diapason of the soprano section is e-f. The text is pleading: "O Lord, may the words of my mouth and the meditation of my heart be acceptable before Thee, Adonay, my Rock and Redeemer." Being the only a cappella piece in the entire composition and pleading as quietly as possible gives it a superb, heavenly atmosphere. Bloch was inspired by the Jewish Sabbath Morning Service and it is generally considered as an equivalent to the Christian mass.

(5) Ruckert actually wrote 448 poems in which his personal grief over the death of his two children was expressed.

(6) There are some exceptional examples, such as Zbigniew Preisner's *Requiem for My Friend,* written in memory of the great film director Krzysztof Kieslowski, who passed away in 1996. Among 19th-century composers of requiems are Cherubini, Berlioz, Dvořák, Bruckner, Verdi, Saint-Saëns, Fauré, and Brahms, with his *Deutsches Requiem,* which is based on German texts and differs from the usual tradition. It should be mentioned that Brahms and Fauré, being agnostic, wrote requiems in a specific style.

(7) Most operas actually deal with basic emotions and issues, which can create drama (love, passion, jealousy, violence, corruption, temptation, faithfulness, death. and more). Some of the music in death scenes can move to tears. For example, in the fourth act of Mussorgsky's *Boris Godunov* (1874), the tsar is losing his mind while approaching his end,

singing, "I am dying." We can hear in the background the voices of the monks who pray for Boris's soul. There are also many other operas that deal with love-life-jealousy-death: Verdi's *Otello* (1887); Puccini's *Tosca* (1900); Debussy's *Pelléas and Mélisande* (1902); Korngold's *Die Tote Stadt (The Dead City)* (1921); and an early opera, Monteverdi's *La Favola D'Orfeo* (1607). Viewing lists of operas shows us that indeed this form of integrative composition is full of death-grief examples. See Hed (1991).

(8) Regarding the connection between music and words, Hirshberg (1974) analyzes the musical expression in early operas such as Monteverdi's *Orfeo* and shows that there is:

- A graphical description of words that mark place and direction (up, down, sun, stars, depth).
- Use of syncopated motives as a rhetoric imitation of excited speech.
- Use of unprepared dissonance to accentuate words expressing pain and despair.
- Musical repetition of words and sentences to accentuate their meaning (pp. 14–16).

Discography

Berlioz, H. (1841–1856). *Summer Nights (Les Nuits d'Été)*. Sony Corporation. Boston Symphony Orchestra. Seiji Ozawa conducting; Frederica von Stade, mezzo-soprano. 2002.

Bernstein, L. (1980) *Halil,* in memory of Yadin Tannenbaum and his soldier-friends. *A Jewish Legacy,* Milken Archive. Asin: BOOOODD77Y. Avner Itai, conductor; Bonita Boyd, flute. 1993.

Bloch, E. (1930–1933). *Sacred Service.* The Zamir chorus of Boston and the Boston Symphony Orchestra in a live concert (personal recording). 1980.

Bruckner, A. (1881). *Symphony No. 7.* Deutsche Grammophon. Wiener Philharmoniker. Herbert von Karajan, conductor. 1990.

Chopin, F. (1937–1939). *Second Piano Sonata, B Flat Minor.* Deutsche Grammophon. Ivo Pogorelich, piano.1981.

Fauré, G. (1887–1888). *Requiem.* Decca record company. Symphony orchestra and choir of Montréal. Charles Dutoit, conductor. 1988.

Fauré, G. (1898). *Suite Opus 80: Pelléas and Mélisande.* Decca record company. Symphony orchestra and choir of Montréal. Charles Dutoit, conductor. 1988.

Mahler, G. (1902). *Kindertotenlieder.* Sony Corporation. Vienna Philharmonic Orchestra. Lorin Maazel, conductor; Agnes Baltsa, mezzo-soprano. 2002.

Monteverdi, C. (1667). *La Favola D'Orfeo.* Lyrichord Discs LEMS 9002. Artek Early Music Ensemble, N.Y. Gwendolyn Toth, director. Christoff and Cluytens, London, 1999.

Penderecki, K. (1967) *Dies Irae—Auschwitz Oratorium.* CHANDOS 9459/60. Chorus and Philharmonic Orchestra of Cracov. Krzysztof Missona, conductor. 1967.

Preisner, Z. (1997–1998) *Requiem for My Friend.* Chester Music. Sinfonia Varsovia with Jacek Kaspszyk; Varsov chamber choir; Elizbieta Towarnicka, soprano. 1998.

Chapter Six

BOBBY LAMENTS HIS GRANDFATHER

A CASE ANALYSIS[1]

"He was gone to the blue land where eagles are red,
cows are green, children are black, and
grandfathers lie deep in the purple earth."
(Bobby, 9 years old)

Dedicated to S. B.[2]

INTRODUCTION

This chapter deals with *Bobby*, an 8-year-old child with severe behavior problems who was brought to music therapy by his parents based on the recommendation of a child psychiatrist. In spite of his problems, Bobby was cooperative from the first moment and demonstrated great love, talent, and creative power through music. He soon brought up many "burning topics" for therapy, among them the issue of his grandfather, who had passed away when Bobby was 6 years old. The subject of death had remained repressed for about two years and had placed the burden of unfinished business on young Bobby's shoulders.

Eventually, due to a conflict with the official educational authorities, the family decided to discontinue all therapies and schooling. Thus, many issues concerning their son were left unsolved.

Music therapy with Bobby continued for about 18 months but never came to a closure, in spite of the fact that the parents perceived and accepted it as a less threatening modality. This is a case analysis, which seemed to be an unfinished symphony, a symphony with a promising beginning and an abrupt conclusion.

Intake

The details I was presented with concerning Bobby were as follows: Bobby was born after a full-term pregnancy. At the age of a few months, he began to show signs of uncontrolled rage and throw temper tantrums, first at home and later at the nursery and elementary school. The school psychologist highly recommended neurological and psychological examinations, but the family was opposed to the idea and denied any problems. Generally speaking, they showed a tendency to blame the system.

The intake process may involve observations on spontaneous or guided music activities. As music engagement influences varied parts of our organism—motion, senses (and sensations), emotion, socialization, cognition, and the integration of parts or all of the abovementioned—it facilitates valuable observational modes. In Bobby's case, I allowed him to freely examine the room and the equipment and intervened when necessary. Bobby immediately moved all over the room, examining the different musical instruments, initiating duets, different manners of playing, etc., as though he had been in music therapy for years. His musical expressions also included the description of different emotional situations, of which the first one was *"splitting."* During the initial intake, splitting was represented by a war between two big-sized instruments: the drum and the cymbal. This interaction, which was solely played by the child, began in a chaotic way with fierce blows, broken rhythmical lines, and shouts. Gradually, from within, without any instructions or suggestions, the music became less chaotic, more patterned and softened. Within a short time, Bobby had dramatically progressed "from ecstasy to relaxation," after which he said the following: "The good cymbal defeated the bad drum, but they won't be friends, neither will they play together." Before leaving, Bobby initiated an additional idea and improvised a song in which the words and music were of his own creation, accompanied on the spot by the therapist:

The Winning Cymbal

"Yes, the cymbal won.
It won over the bad
And that is that!"

(Your song is beautiful)
"Many thanks."
(And your voice is pretty)
"So are the flowers."

This song of praise was indeed sung softly, with a natural flow of a tonal melody in F major and in a beautiful clear voice.

It was very difficult to gather from his singing that this was the child whom kids in school had nicknamed "the Devil." On the contrary, one could sense the "Angel" within Bobby's psyche. The splitting between bad and good that Bobby presented in his symbolic playing actually reflected his personality. In the music therapy clinic, he tended to show the Good Bobby, while in school and at home he attacked children and teachers with stones and knives. Thus the intake-observational session, which became the first therapeutic hour, concluded with the song that described the content of the events.

Therapeutic Considerations

The reports I received from the school and the psychiatrist drew a picture of a very troubled child: Due to conflicts with the educational system, Bobby's parents had moved him as a young child from one nursery school to another. This situation made it very difficult to develop ongoing bonds, and, indeed, Bobby was a friendless child who suffered from loneliness.

In addition, he failed in coping with academic requirements. He was not able to concentrate, and although his intelligence was found to be normal, at the age of 8 he could not read, write, or calculate. He endangered his surroundings with his aggressive behavior, was on the edge of being removed from school, and was referred to special education. In public elementary school, the child was diagnosed as having:

- Organically Based Development Disorder
- Impulsive-unpredictable behavior
- Uncontrolled anger
- Overwhelming fantasies and anxiety
- Impaired reality judgment
- Unstable-instense interpersonal relationship
- Low self-image
- Underachievement in school
- No learning disabilities
- Poor verbal communication
- Normal motor development

SPLITTING. The splitting mechanism was presented in our first meeting and appeared again several times during the 18 months of music therapy. Splitting was defined by Freud (1938) as "The two contrary reactions to the conflict persist as the centerpoint of a split in the ego" (p. 372). Laplanche and Portalis (1985) defined this term as: "The coexistence at the heart of the ego of two psychical attitudes toward external reality insofar as this stands in the way of an instinctual demand. The first of these attitudes takes reality into consideration, while the second disavows it and replaces it by a product of desire" (p. 427). Melanie Klein (1989) described splitting as the most primitive kind of defense mechanism against anxiety. According to her, it may involve the object and the ego. In the course of normal development, the child learns to integrate the good and the bad object. In cases where splitting and disintegration occur frequently, the child is liable to develop emotional problems (as in Bobby's case) and in the future have relationship problems and exhibit obscure judgment concerning intimacy (Siegel & Spellman, 2002). As for the tantrums mentioned, in her 83rd session of a child analysis, Klein writes: "I believe that tantrums always contain despair as well, because while the rage and attacks go on, the child feels that he is more and more irreparably destroying the loved person, particularly his internalized one" (p. 423).

As mentioned, different expressions of splitting emerged throughout the two years of music therapy, but at this initial stage I asked myself whether symbolizing the splitting through music could serve as a preliminary step for elaboration. All of this already arising as part of the intake process gave me some hope.

Family Secrets

MUTISM. Bobby's parents brought him regularly to music therapy, probably because they felt less threatened by this modality, but also because they understood that Bobby's love for music might serve as a channel for a more normalized expression. Indeed, this was true for most of the sessions, but at times Bobby was extremely disturbed by the fact that his parents demanded he conceal information from the schoolteacher, from the music therapist, and from others. This dual loyalty, which deepened the existing splitting, confused Bobby to the point of temporary mutism, as seen in the following examples:

> Bobby came to therapy, sat near the door in an embryo posture, and did not utter a word. I decided to sit on the carpet with my guitar, singing, describing and reflecting to him what he was doing and how difficult it must be to keep silent. It took half an hour before Bobby showed any reaction. He very slowly progressed on his bottom, came nearby and showed signs of visual communication. At that moment, I composed a little song into which we would be able to cast our own words. The melody served as a basic container, and I began to sing. After one verse, Bobby joined in, and it became an improvised continuation of changing roles. From the words that sprang forth, I could deduce that he was not allowed to tell about a certain event that had occurred at home. When the session ended, Bobby was relaxed, said good-bye quietly, and departed.

From the moment Bobby began to react, the verbal improvisation was:

> T. Your leg is moving slowly
> Moving to the rhythm of the music
> Your mouth is strictly closed
> It is very difficult to keep mute
> It is very difficult to stop singing.
> B. mmmmm strictly closed …
> *(I encourage him by the same humming voices, and he begins to sing:)*
> B. One day Bobby was numb and very sad
> He could not tell why he had to keep his mouth shut,
> and he wanted only music for his heart.
> T. I'll sing a song for you, Bobby,
> I'll sing for your sad heart and try to help it.
> B. I cannot tell why I am shutting my words in the prison. It is a secret, a little secret, and it can be dangerous to tell it.
> T. It is allowed to keep secrets. You have the right not to tell.
> B. But I'll tell it to my bear, I'll only share it with my bear, and I try to be musical.
> T. And you are very successful in being musical.
> B. You are right.
> T. It is a good feeling to succeed.
> B. It is a good feeling that you are successful. So I'll stay here till midnight.

There was no question about several issues concerning these family secrets: Bobby was under intense pressure. The parents, who resisted consultation, were damaging the child by their demands. The child chose to solve the conflict by "shutting himself up," hoarding loads of sadness and aggressiveness. Bergman and Cohen (1994) explain that each family has unwritten rules that supervise the inner and external stream of information. The demand on the child to keep secrets, and the denial of the family concerning the danger in doing so, places a burden on the child's mind and heart. The results may surface in pathological behavior (aggressive or passive). In Bobby's case, though the diagnosis was based on organic development, this factor certainly added psychological undertones to the general picture.

While playing for Bobby during his muteness, I recalled the Moroccan medicine man who visits the patient's house and plays on his rita (Moroccan oboe) different ariah (short "amulet" melodies) in order to find the Jin (devil) that caused the malady, and through it to cure the patient (Sekeles, 1996/1997). The search for the right melody and words require of the healer intense focus on the patient and the need to remain calm and not elicit extra pressure. In a way, all of these originate from the same therapeutic category. Added to this is the fact that the melody was repetitive and somehow acted as a "melodic amulet." It also occurred to me that in the Hebrew language, mutism = elem, and violence = alimut — both are derived from the same grammatical root. Indeed, both situations may represent the extreme manifestations of the same origin. In his everyday life, Bobby mainly employed violence and at times mutism. In music therapy, he used only organized violence, namely through his improvised songs and his drumming. During the elaboration process, it had become obvious that Bobby had aggressive fantasies toward himself as well as toward his parents. When anger and violence were channeled into the physical action of drumming, he was able to achieve better organization and sublimation.

Lamentations

Bobby's grandfather, with whom he had had a warm relationship, had passed away. Unfortunately, his death had been kept in the domain of family secrets and was neither discussed at home nor explained to his grandchild. This was another stress factor that kept Bobby from overcoming his problems and ventilating his overflooded head and heart. This burden was revealed in music therapy through several cases of improvised lamentations:

1. Bobby entered the room, took a soprano recorder, sat on the carpet, opened it, began to move forward and backward as in a Jewish prayer, put a tiny doll inside the recorder, closed it, and sang in an incantation prayer style: "Saba (Grandpa) was sick and died. Saba was never buried. He probably disappeared into the air. No, he went away to the blue land where eagles are red, cows are green, children are black, and grandfathers lie deep in the purple earth."

2. During another session, Bobby took a Chinese box, wrapped it in a piece of cotton, placed it beneath the huge timpani, and improvised a drumming ceremony for the dead. His drumming was harsh but rhythmically well organized, and its grave spirit was reminiscent of a funeral march.

3. Bobby took a black piece of paper and a white color. He filled the entire space with tiny white figures in different directions and postures. After finishing his painting, he folded it into a thin scroll, placed it inside the piano, and said: "Now you'll play for my grandpa because he loves music so much, and I'll sing for him." I improvised a semi-lullaby melody and Bobby immediately joined in with the following words: "Relax, Grandpa, I am guarding you. You disappeared, but nobody told me you had died. I know you are dead. I know because you were my best friend. Relax. Grandpa, I won't tell your secret."

Therapeutic Considerations

To the domain of family secrets was now added the blurring of grandfather's death and its denial by the parents in their son's presence. They never discussed the grandfather's death with Bobby and were certain that he did not possess the ability to understand the meaning of death and that it would accentuate his fear and anxiety with regard to the topic.

Many parents, specifically those of older generations, shared the idea that the facts of death might damage their young children, as they (the parents) did not possess the psychological tools to cope with this issue. In a way, it was treated as taboo, similar to the subject of sex. In his research, Kastenbaum (1974) reported that in answering a questionnaire he distributed, more than three-fourths of the participants shared the opinion that children "are better off not thinking of death and should be protected from death-relevant situations by their parents" (p. 12). Smilansky (1981) suggested the following points in adult support for grieving children:

- Relaying the facts in a language suiting the child's development.
- Easing the grief by "being with" the children.
- Emotional and cognitive elaboration on the facts and adaptation of a new reality.
- Constructing a new reality.
- Discussing the dead person and letting the child express his feelings toward the dead.
- Showing understanding of the child's wishes.
- Alleviating future worries (p. 94).

In Bobby's life, none of the aforementioned was done, and he probably experienced many black, frightening holes in his inner and outer existence. Creating symbolic rituals concerning death and playing with it through varied artistic variations and modalities were the first signs of grieving for his grandfather and a proper entry through the gate of elaboration work. It is important to remember that Bobby initiated all this by himself, most likely when he felt accepted and able to trust the therapist.

Bobby's parents used denial and resistance as defense mechanisms and were unable to supply their son with "holding" and safety. Superficially, the family maintained a normal façade. However, sometimes a thick layer of frustration and anger burst through.

The role of grandparents in family life is discussed in literature, including that of grandparents to children with physical disability. On the other hand, the loss of grandparents is seldom mentioned or dealt with in depth. In practice, we may observe many children for whom the grandparent held the role of a holding figure, facilitating the unconditional love of a supporter. This occurs specifically when the parents have difficulties filling these roles, endangering the child to the point of becoming a "child at risk." At present, grandfathers (like fathers) have assumed new roles that encompass nurturing, affection, being playful companions, and acting as a listening ear rather than being an authoritarian figure as used to be the case in the past (Anderson, Tunaley, & Walker, 2000). Bobby sensed and remembered his grandfather as a friend, as a fun-loving person and as a play partner.[3] The silence surrounding his disappearance and the fact that he never had the chance to mourn for him created a heavy burden on his tiny shoulders. In the music therapy room, he could for the first time access his grief, act it out, and work through it. After creating several mourning rituals as described above, Bobby was ready to talk straightforwardly about death. I requested of the parents to take him to the cemetery but received a negative reaction mixed with anger, due to the fact that the child dared to deal with such a subject in the music room. I realized that the parents did not yet accept the role of music as a therapeutic tool and that the several meetings I had had with them had not served to accomplish the intentioned results.

Bobby worked for more than half a year on the death of his grandfather, the anxiety he felt, his loneliness, and his desire to be less aggressive in school. He composed songs, used the theater dolls to tell his invented stories, and along the way began to use writing in order to put the recorded songs on paper. Bobby was not compelled by me to do so, and this occurred spontaneously. I sensed that he might be proud of the fact that I was keeping all of his creations (musical recordings, written songs, paintings) in a special file and that he could look at it from time to time. He was a clever boy not with learning disabilities but rather with emotional obstacles, prone to attacks of rage that prevented him from developing normally. Nevertheless, when he was contented, he discovered his natural abilities, and his musical success aided him in his progress in general academic studies.

More Splitting

As aforementioned, Bobby portrayed the issue of splitting through different modalities. The following examples show how he imagined himself through the pictures he painted with the aid of music of his choice:

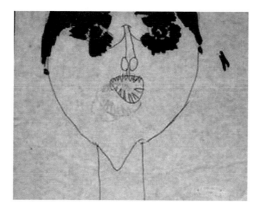

THE BAD ME

This was his first self-portrait, done with a black felt pen. He went over the eyes again and again, blackening them as much as possible. He drew the nose in the shape of a penis and the mouth possibly like a vulva and explained: "This is the Bad Me."

A week later, he again drew a self-portrait and explained: "Me, the Wrecker. My eyes are shooting laser beams, my nose is sending a rocket, and fire shoots out of my mouth."

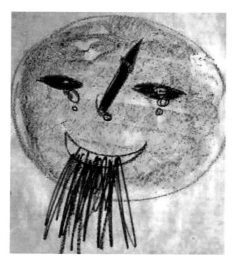

ME, THE WRECKER

Four months later, after intensive work elaborating on the subject of self-image, a new image emerged: "The Good Me." In this painting, we see a crowned king dressed in bright colors. Indeed, Bobby's self image had begun to change. At the same time, his behavior in school improved and became less aggressive. His parents were more cooperative, though still very suspicious, and Bobby began to talk openly about his topsy-turvy world, his loneliness, the unpredictability in his life, his immense longing for his grandfather figure and more. At that time, he composed a song on his topsy-turvy world and painted the following:

THE GOOD ME

The next painting was completed when he listened to "The Golden Voyage," mainly composed of birds' singing and the sound of waterfalls. It was of mother eagle flying in the air carrying her two babies on her back. Bobby clarified: "The picture is from the land of scribbles and dreams. The two babies and their mother are flying through the air, never able to descend to earth. At worst, if the chicks are tired, they can rest on their mother's back—that is, if she agrees to slow down a bit."

With these words, Bobby expressed several things: his wish to descend to a safe place, to live down-to-earth, and his difficulty with his mother's unpredictability. The eagle is known as a strong, large bird. The little babies are very small, and there is a third one that looks as though he had fallen or remained alone in the high sky. The music played throughout seemed to facilitate a safe atmosphere and may have helped Bobby control his frightening fantasies. Bobby was now at a stage where he was ready to speak about his problems, though he needed a lot more time and work to become stabilized and to bring the extremities of his emotional world closer together.

MOTHER EAGLE

EPILOGUE

Due to a decision made by the educational authorities to involve the Child Psychological Service in Bobby's academic future, the family decided to sever all contacts, perhaps due to their fear of the suggested special education framework. In music therapy, I was given one hour for this sudden departure, throughout which the child was crying most of the time. It was nearly impossible to inject a word. I was simply there with Bobby. Miri, the child from chapter 1, was lucky to have a mature father and the positive involvement of grandparents. These aspects had helped her to use music therapy in an efficient way. Bloom (1964), Anastasiow

(1985), and Erez (1993) consider the parental maturity essential for enhancing the development of children at risk and comment that maturity is not directly related to the adult's age, intelligence, or socioeconomic status. Bobby's parents held academic professions and had their own perspectives on life and health. The minute someone tried to guide them or to suggest a different approach, they felt threatened. Stein and Avidan (1992), in their analysis of *Unconscious Efforts of Parents to Preserve the Psychopathology of their Offspring,* found in such families the following features:

- Extreme rigidity
- Enmeshment within the family
- Inability to solve conflicts and diminish the level of emotionality
- Polarity between the parents
- Highly expressed emotions of hostility toward the system

These points are quite adequate for the case at hand. On the whole, in spite of the difficulties Bobby had in the course of his development, he succeeded in expressing and elaborating on his splitting and ambivalent feelings through art and verbal means. He was able to drum out his anger and progressed from extreme violence to a soft, gentle creativity. In some of his songs, he even revealed a sense of humor, being able to make jokes about himself. But he was not granted enough time to conclude the process and was not given the chance to overcome his behavioral problems the way he wished to, as he had expressed in the following song:

> *This is what I like to do in class: To mess around, to bother everyone, to break the teacher's head. That's the "bad me," but there is also a "good me." Sometimes the "bad me" beats the "good me." Sometimes the "good me" beats the "bad me." One day, the "bad me" is going to explode. It will explode like a volcano, and its buttocks will be blown up like a balloon, and the "good me" will be left alone. He'll be calm, he'll be calm.*

Notes

(1) This case analysis is based on a short version that was published under a different name and accentuation in the *Niewsbrief B.M.T. Tweede Jaargang,* Editie Mei, 2000, pp. 18–26.

(2) S. B. immigrated to Israel from Italy in the forties as an adolescent, leaving his family abroad. He finished high school and graduated as a sculptor from the academy of art. In addition to his studies and creative work, he used to volunteer and successfully aid children in his neighborhood who suffered from behavior disturbances. In his mid-twenties, he fell ill with brain cancer that could not be operated on or cured. Within a few months, his condition deteriorated and he passed away. This chapter is dedicated to him, to his artistic energy, and to his wonderful model of investment in children.

(3) A few examples from my clinical work concerning the meaning of grandparents to children: O. U. was born as a Down's syndrome child and was in music therapy throughout his entire childhood. At a certain point, he decided to learn to play the piano and was very decisive about it. He recently said to me: "Do you know why I must play the piano and be very diligent? Because my grandma who died and whom I loved very much was a piano teacher and I want to follow her footsteps. This is why." D. I., a 12-year-old girl whose grandfather had died of cancer, told me the following: "When my grandpa was sick in bed, I came to visit him every day. I kissed him and prayed to God to help him die without pain because he was my best friend and we all loved him very much. It helped because he had a kiss death." (A "kiss death" in Hebrew means a death without suffering: the death of a holy person.)

Chapter Seven

TO BE AFRAID OF YOUR OWN SHADOW

A CASE ANALYSIS

"He will destroy death forever;
and the Lord God will wipe away tears from off all faces;
and the rebuke of His people shall He take away from off all the earth,
for the Lord hath spoken it."
(Isaiah 25:8)

Dedicated to Meir Harnik[1]

INTRODUCTION

Avi suffered from both neurological dysfunction and psychological traumas. He dwelt with his family in a settlement behind "The Green Line"[2] and exhibited severe anxieties, which prevented him from doing many simple activities such as playing in the backyard of his home. Avi had five brothers and two sisters. He was the sixth-born. Because of his neurological dysfunction, mild retardation, and learning disabilities, his studies took place in the city, in a special education school. This necessitated a daily bus drive back and forth. During these journeys, he used to sit frozen in his seat and at times cry out in anxiety. At the age of seven, he was referred to music therapy by the school's psychological advisor. Throughout the two and a half years that Avi was in therapy, it became obvious that a great number of his anxieties were a result of the many losses the family had suffered and the possibly dangerous experiences of his everyday reality. If I had to draw a line recounting Avi's development in music therapy, I would do the following:

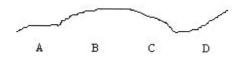

A is the first half-year of therapy, in which the child learned to use music for expression, representations, fun, and relaxation.

B is the sessions during which he began to speak openly of the losses and anxieties he experienced.

C is the elaboration period, in which we worked very actively on the anxiety-eliciting subjects.

D is group therapy and conclusion.

Intake and Observation

- *Observation location*—Well-equipped music therapy clinic.

- *Duration/date/hour*—

- *Reported to*—

- *Received by*—

- *Name of patient*—Avi (changed for ethical reasons)

- *Age*—7 years old.

- *Address*—

- *Educational framework*—Special education school

- *Family*—Parents and eight children

- *Reason for referral to music therapy*—Neuropsychological condition of child: mild retardation, learning disabilities, and psychologically based anxieties

- *Previous and present therapeutic frameworks*—None

- *Diagnosis*—Mild retardation, learning disabilities, and psychologically based anxieties

- *External impression*—A sweet, polite child, very cooperative, eager to be a "good boy," has some vision problems and mild hyperactivity

- *Equipment employed*—None

- *Movement (fine and gross mobility)*—General hypotonia, head and torso lean forward, left side is dominant, changes posture every few minutes. He accompanies his talking with energetic movements and while listening moves in back and forth, praying movements. Avi has difficulties in finger separation and in directing his hands in an efficient way (apraxis).

- *Senses*—Hearing seems to be normal, has some vision problems (as yet unclear)

- *Vocality*—Avi speaks and sings very willingly. His speech is very quick, not always fluent, but understandable. His singing is clear, and he keeps tonality easily. He is able to improvise within a harmonic frame and adds words from time to time. His pronunciation of words while singing is very clear compared to his nonmelodic speech.

- *Rhythmicality*—Both rhythmical perception and rhythmical performance are very good. His muscle tone is elevated while drumming with both hands.

- *Instrument playing*—He moves quickly from one instrument to the other, drumming with two hands in a free, creative way. In four-hands piano playing, he tries to cooperate in spite of his fine motor difficulties. Avi enjoys conversing through the piano. While playing simple wind instruments he invests too much energy in order to produce a sound and while doing so stiffens his neck muscles.

- *Hearing and listening*—Seem normal

- *Emotional aspects*—Avi is an energetic, hyperactive child, verbally and musically communicative, interested in contact. He tries to be a good child and to overcome his concentration difficulties. He tells stories with tragic contents but is not ready to discuss them and abandons them as soon as possible.

- *Cognitive aspects*—Avi has associative thinking. As he becomes excited, his sentence formation becomes chaotic and so does his pronunciation. He can only read with punctuations. His mathematical abilities are low for his age.

- *Social aspects*—Avi is very cooperative when interacting with an adult. Generally speaking, he is a very lonely child and has no socialization strategies. This fact contributes to his closing up at home as a result of anxiety.

- *Summary and recommendations*—Avi seems to be a very easy child to be with, but at the moment he probably needs a period of adaptation and to form a trusting relationship before he'll be able to seriously work on his anxieties and loneliness. As he loves music and is ready to use it in different creative ways, I believe that it would be worthwhile to proceed with developmental-integrative music therapy that takes into consideration the physical, emotional, cognitive, and social aspects of development.

Therapeutic Considerations

Avi was raised in a loving family that acted as a small community within a larger community. His parents were very intelligent and aware of their son's need for help. At home and perhaps in their community as well, people did not discuss their emotional problems and were very busy building the country according to their own principles and beliefs. Through my work with children whose parents have strong idealistic principles concerning Israel, I have noticed that parents attempt to bequeath these principles to their children, usually with great success. There are several problems inherent in this process: 1. Not every child is strong enough to cope with the existential dangers that accompany certain ideologies. In this case, Avi, due to his developmental problems, was unable to do so. 2. The conversations surrounding idealistic issues do not include clarification of emotional content. Avi was not accustomed to talking about his difficulties and certainly not used to asking for help. Neither was he encouraged to do so by his parents. They loved him and took care of him, and in practice he was also helped by his brothers and sisters. However, when he was frightened and unable to function, the family encouraged him to overcome his feelings and to behave normally. They would request that he employ a form of detachment mechanism, but he could not do so as he was overwhelmed by anxiety. Each time the radio/television informed the public of a terror attack or shooting or wounding of civilians, he had proof that the dangers were not imagined. They were real. Yet when Avi's situation became very difficult, they decided to bring him to music therapy, as music was his beloved art.

It became clear to me that treating Avi was not enough and that I would have to find a way to change the parents' attitude and help them understand that the child's anxiety could be worked on only through a mutual collaboration. In order to do so, I suggested a monthly meeting to clarify the developmental progress and the general situation. The parents immediately consented.

A. Music Therapy First Stage (about six months)

This stage was characterized by experimenting with musical improvisations in different ways: Avi tried out the many musical instruments, learned to converse through music in interactions with the therapist, experienced activating songs from different categories (motor, sensory, emotional, cognitive, and social), sang, was stimulated by music to move and paint, listened to short compositions, created music for his little theatrical stories, and, in spite of his difficulties, began to write little songs.

Generally speaking, Avi had improved his motor skills throughout this stage and was taught to elevate his muscle tone through proper movement. He extended his concentration span and experienced much pleasure. Avi began to trust the therapist and to understand that music can express emotions. I regard this period as an introductory warming up phase for the impending developments. During this phase, we planted the roots of the music therapy process.

PARENT-THERAPIST MEETINGS. Throughout this stage, I met the

parents approximately once a month, and we had conversations concerning Avi's development and needs as well as some experiences with music. Avi was not present in these meetings. Though it could not be defined under the title of Family Therapy, I did use some of my acquired knowledge of the field. In their first chapter, "In Search of the Golden Mean," Bergman and Cohen (1994) write that regarding each child in the family, the parents must ask themselves: How much pressure can be put on the child? Can I trust his ability to make decisions? Do we have to expose him to such a reality, and how much protection and help should we provide? Concerning education and growth, parents are naturally inclined to behave in accordance with their personality, beliefs and ideals. The encounter with the child's response sometimes compels them to recheck their strategies and mobilize themselves to alter them.

In our first conversation, I told them of Avi's musical creativity and expressed hope that based on it we would be able to help him. We agreed that concern for Avi's well-being was what should guide them as parents and me as his therapist. We also agreed that Avi was different from their other children and that he may require a special, adapted attitude. They claimed that by principle they treated him as equal to their other children, and we discussed the possibility of changing this philosophy for Avi's sake. Generally speaking, the meetings in this first stage progressed slowly, with no dramatic developments, but they gradually proved efficient.

B and C. Music Therapy Second Stage (about 12 months)

From these stages, I chose three examples, which will be presented in chronological order. It should be mentioned that these examples are but a few out of many others.

1. The Bloody Bus

Avi came to the session and told me that he had had a dream—a nightmare. He requested to draw his dream, and the picture below was the result. His explanation: "I went to school on a bus full of many other children. Suddenly, I heard a very, very terrible noise like the voice of a thousand witches, and the whole bus flew in the air. Only the floor, which was covered with blood, remained. All the children were dead and flew out of the windows. I lost my hands and legs and could never move again." He then added: "This is why I'll never again ride on a bus."

We worked further on the subject through verbal discussion, shifting to music and recounting the dream through musical improvisations, finding the most important scenes in the dream and so on. It was clear to me that soothing is primal and not the way to treat Avi's severe anxiety. On the other hand, it was also unclear whether the artistic modalities (painting, music) and the verbal discussions were doing the work. Nonetheless, these were the events that took place in the described session and I decided to wait patiently for more developments.

2. The Death March

Several weeks later, Avi entered the music therapy room, sat by the piano, and began to sing an incessant mourning song in an incantation style in which he named and told the story of all of the people his family and the community had lost in the past years. While chanting, he rhythmically hit the piano's keys and at a certain moment asked me to accompany him. I did so by slowly playing contours, perceiving his singing as a recitative, thus supporting him. This musical occurrence was experienced as a march of dead people in a long, endless row. Later on, I obtained information from the family that supplied proof that all of the names and stories were true.

Avi had stored in his memory everything that he had heard about death and tragedies in his community and family. It was as though he had collected mounds of details that contributed to his anxiety. How do we work on anxiety when real life is the main contributor to its origin? How was it possible to support Avi without changing his environment, his community, and his country? How could I make him stronger, considering the fact that he was born with neurological problems and mild retardation?

3. An Artistic Cemetery

Throughout a long period, Avi established burial ceremonies through every artistic modality. He commenced the entire process by choosing a big cardboard box in which he asked me to store his future creations. He began with paintings of different motives that indeed are typical of Jewish cemeteries[3]: mainly the Star of David, the blessing hands, and a cut-off tree. He painted several variations on these topics and did not talk of their meanings. I knew that he was acquainted with the cemetery near his village. He proceeded by taking a plastic box of butter, painting it with colors, and placing something inside. He then closed it and scattered some earth on it. He then placed it in the cardboard box and asked me to keep it in the music room, declaring that it was a cemetery.

I sensed that by doing so, he was coping with his death anxiety through action. I asked Avi for permission to invite his parents to one of his music therapy sessions, with the notion that it might help them better understand what frightens him. Avi agreed.

4. Drumming the Bad People to Death

Avi was a gentle child who rarely exerted strength, not even while drumming. I tried to encourage him to do so by playing together and supplying modeling or by playing along with precomposed drumming or as a reaction to a story. It worked somewhat, until Avi fully recognized the possibility of making a lot of noise and initiated a story: "There once was a bad man who killed one person every day. So he killed children, fathers and mothers, grandfathers and grandmothers, uncles and aunts, animals, and everything. Then he hid the dead people in a cave in the mountains and put a huge stone at its entrance. One day, a group of children passed by the cave and found all the dead people. They ran away and called the police and the soldiers. The man was captured and put in prison forever." After he told this horror story, he began to beat the orchestral timpani with all of his might. It should be mentioned that at Avi's home there was no television, so this "film" was his personal invention and the product of his imagination. Up until the hour's end, we worked together just on beating the huge drums, chasing away the ghosts and frightening evils that filled Avi's heart and head.

Through his story, just as through the "bloody bus" painting, Avi was able to open a window into the frightening pictures in his mind that caused his unbearable anxiety. Expressing the themes fueling his anxiety through artistic modalities and explaining them with words added additional value to the entire process, compared with just talking. As a music therapist, I frequently feel that this is one of the strongest advantages our profession has to offer.

Generally speaking, anxiety is defined as "… a state of uneasiness, accompanied by dysphoria and somatic signs and symptoms of tension, focused on apprehension of possible failure, misfortune, or danger" (Colman, p. 46). In Avi's case, the threat of danger was real. The community's philosophy of "God shall guard us and we have to be strong" was not relevant to Avi. He was not strong and he was not mature enough to understand his community's ideology. Salvador Minuchin (1974) explains that in most societies, the family stamps self-values and individuality on its members. Experiencing human identification has two aspects: the sense of belonging and the sense of separation. The sense of belonging is developed within the family's boundaries, and the sense of separation develops as a result of participation in subfamilial settings and in extrafamilial groups and relationships. Avi essentially had a strong, almost compelling sense of belonging without the strength that it might facilitate. He had not, however, exercised separation or parting because of his loneliness and communication difficulties. The meetings with the parents revolved around this concept, and I hoped that the parents would alter their attitude and support their son in every possible way. Indeed, due to their goodwill the changes eventually transpired, and Avi's self-confidence improved. In therapy, we dedicated part of the hour to socialization until it became apparent that Avi needed group therapy.

Group music therapy is an important branch in our profession. It has been employed from ancient times on, as in healing rituals of traditional societies such as Siberia (Sekeles, 2000). Group music therapy has become the topic of much theoretical research (Plach, 1980; Davies & Richards, 2002; Pavlicevic, 2003; Hunt, 2005).

5. Social Interaction

The group was composed of four children about Avi's age (7 to 8): a blind boy, a girl who suffered from spina bifida, another girl with learning disabilities, and Avi. Virginia Satir (1989) mentions four life aspects are ever present in family dynamics:

- Self-esteem (the feelings and thoughts that a person develops in connection to himself)
- Communication (the paths people choose in order to create interrelationships)
- The family structure (the rules people use to direct their feelings and actions)
- Social contacts (the interrelationships between family members and the outside world)

I decided to work on these four life aspects within the group. Through music, it was possible to establish clear rules that were flexible enough to leave place for the expression of individual wishes. We exercised interrelationships through different musical techniques that also helped to encourage the children to demonstrate patience and respect for one another. Self-confidence and self-esteem were developed through these approaches. The group therapy stage continued for a year, and at its end, the music therapy process was concluded.

SUMMARY

Avi, a 7-year-old boy at that time, was brought to music therapy with the following problems: mild retardation, learning disabilities, hypotonia, lack of social skills, and anxiety that sabotaged his everyday life.

Avi lived with his family in a community outside "the Green Line" whose members had experienced many tragedies, including death, injuries, and more. He went to school every day in an armored bus, but still feared his own shadow, a fact that did not promote his development of social strategies.

Being one of eight children, Avi was educated, as all of his brothers and sisters were, in light of a specific ideology that accentuated the positive sides of being strong and which related to God's will. Avi was too weak to exercise this direction. It should be stressed that Avi's parents and family were caring, loving people with strong faith in their chosen path. In spite of this faith, they agreed to meet with the therapist monthly and gradually, as far as Avi was concerned, shifted their inflexible ideology to one more comforting and supporting.

With Avi's permission, the parents also joined two of their son's sessions. The fact that music possesses all of the curing aspects of "playing" (not only the fun, but also the ability to discharge anger, aggressiveness, and anxiety, and to develop human relationships, socialization, and communication) helped all those involved and certainly illustrated to the parents their son's world of frightening fantasies. As Winnicott (1971) formulated it: "The natural thing is playing, and the highly sophisticated 20th-century phenomenon is psychoanalysis. It must be of value to the analyst to be constantly reminded not only of what is owed to Freud but also of what we owe to the natural and universal thing called playing" (p. 48). The power of playing through music proved true in regard to Avi himself, Avi and his parents, Avi and the therapist, and Avi and the therapeutic group.

Music therapy was the modality through which Avi began to express himself, his anxieties, his horror fantasies, and his loneliness. Following 18 months of individual music therapy, in order to encourage

Avi's communication and socialization, I formed a group of four children who spent a year together exercising human relationships. At the end of this period, Avi's process was concluded and the music therapy sessions were discontinued.

Frequently, adults do their best to mold the lives of their children in accordance to their own beliefs, ideologies, and education. Children often do their best to follow their parents' lead in order to gain their parents' approval and acceptance and to feel part of a group or a community and share a common power. In the case of children who suffer from deficiencies, this may prove to be a dangerous tendency. It may eventually operate as an obstacle and disrupt the child's development. Avi was lucky to have parents with goodwill and enough strength to work on and accept change, thereby saving their son from further deterioration. Among other alterations, one of them began to accompany Avi on the bus, encouraging and supporting him by remaining near to him, and gradually improving his self-confidence.

The Muslim claims that we cannot change our fate, that it is fixed from birth on and that death will arrive whenever Allah (God) has appointed it. I wonder about this fatalistic saying. Even so, 11 years later, Avi was killed in a car accident and was buried in the graveyard near his village. God bless his soul.

Notes

(1) Meir Harnik was born in 1927 and died in a motorcycle accident in 1972. He was an excellent musician, a performing pianist, a choir director, a presenter of programs in the Israeli radio, among the initiators of the Israeli television, and a creator of songs as well as of piano compositions. He traveled all over the country with his vocal group to present Israeli songs and encouraged the careers of many young artists. I dedicate this chapter to Meir Harnik for his multifaceted, colorful personality and for his musical friendship and inspiration.

(2) "The Green Line" is the term given to the border of Israel as was established by the 1949 armistice agreement with Jordan. This transpired before the Six Days War (1967) in which Israel conquered the West Bank and Gaza. Most countries and organizations view the green line as a de facto border.

(3) Incantation is a vocal style that includes melodic speech and spells. It can be found in the healing rituals of traditional societies and in Western music of mystical content (see Sekeles, 1995).

(4) The ornamentation on Israeli-Jewish gravestones is traditionally limited. For example: *the Star of David* = shield of David. This six-pointed star has held meaning in Judaism since the 6th century B.C.E. and symbolizes the reconciliation of opposites. It is seen on tombstones, in synagogues, and on the Israeli flag. *Hands* held in benediction is the symbol of the Cohen = the priestly family of the Levi's tribe. *A crown* is a symbol of the "Torah" (the first part of the Bible) or of priesthood, kings, or God. *Animals: The lion* is the symbol of Judah's tribe; *the deer* is the symbol of Naftali's tribe. *A lamp with seven candles* symbolizes wisdom and purification. *A cut-off tree* is the symbol of a cut-off life. (Robertson, 2006.) Due to Avi's traditional education, he was probably familiar with some of these symbols from his family and community.

Chapter Eight

MOTHER, THE WHITE DOVE

A CASE ANALYSIS

"I tell you, Mother. I feel sad, but cannot cry. I feel angry, but cannot
scream. I am rotten, but I cannot purify myself. I am doomed."
(Jonas, 12th session)

Dedicated to Reuven Morgan[1]

INTRODUCTION

The eighth chapter, "Mother, the White Dove" describes and analyzes
Jonas, a young man in his early twenties, whose mother died of cancer
following a long period of sickness. Jonas was diagnosed as suffering
from Borderline Personality Disorder[2] and resisted verbal therapy. He
agreed to participate in music therapy, assuming that he might
circumvent speech and have fun.

As art therapists, terms and idioms from the art itself frequently
accompany our observations and therapeutic considerations, such as a
Sonata Form or, in the present case, an Expressionistic Style. Jonas used
"expressionistic" symbolism prompted by music and other modalities that
ultimately helped him cope with the shadows of the past.

Before proceeding with the actual case study, I will provide some
background on the concept of expressionistic symbolism, which constituted
an integral part of the therapeutic process. This concept is intended to
highlight a form of expression frequently observed in music therapy:
externalization of emotionally loaded issues through broad dynamics,
accelerated tempo, and dense tones sounds, which are analogous to
expressionistic visual art.

What Is Expressionism?

In general, "expressionism" is a creative style in different cultures, which accentuates, maximizes, and distorts reality in order to highlight the symbolic or intrinsic meaning of an object, e.g., grotesque masks used by Native North Americans for healing rituals or war. The features of these masks were maximized, often to the point of frightening distortions that were meant to ward away evil spirits. This was in light of the magical-tribal thinking that "like acts on like" (Avneyon, 2005). Specifically, expressionism refers to a Western artistic movement (1863–1944) that aimed to highlight the emotional meaning hidden in an external representation, i.e., to express the outer world through the subjective view of the artist (Gombrich, 1971; Laurent, 2004). Alexey von Javlensky wrote in *Der Blaue Reiter* that the expressionist artist expresses only what he has within himself, not what he sees with his eyes (Javlensky, 1948).

The following characteristics typify expressionistic art: intense colors that are not necessarily natural, dense textures, sharp transitions, and distortions. On the whole, expressionism tended to describe the ugly, embarrassing, grotesque, and painful. Emil Nolde expressed his feelings concerning the classical techniques in the following way: "Conscientious and exact imitation of nature does not create a work of art" (Chipp, 1971, p. 146). An excellent example of this style was found in an exhibition entitled "A Psychoanalytic Portrait" by the Czech artist Kokoschka. The exhibition, held in Vienna in 1908, presented a character portrait that highlighted eye expressions and hand structures. This is the antithesis of traditional art, which typically attempts to idealize reality. The expressionist movement has often been stigmatized as representing decadence; the Nazis went so far as to ban it and persecute expressionist artists. Adolph Hitler said that anybody who painted and saw a green sky and blue pastures out to be sterilized (Chipp, 1971).

The term "expressionism" has been metaphorically adapted from the visual arts to the context of music. Expressionistic music is written in a deeply subjective and introspective style. The most renowned expressionistic musical compositions are Schönberg's *Verklärte Nacht* and *Pierrot Lunaire,* as well as Berg's operas *Lulu* and *Wozzeck* (Austin, 1966; Griffiths, 1986). Why use the term "expressionism" in relation to Jonas? I will attempt to clarify the answer.

Intake

Jonas provided the following information about himself during our first meeting: He was born and raised in a village. When he was 11 years old, his mother was diagnosed with cancer. She stayed in the small family home for four years until she died of her illness. Jonas dropped out of high school and was discharged prematurely from the army on account of unsuitability. He began music therapy because he found it difficult to cooperate in the process of verbal psychotherapy. As he put it, he was willing to make a serious effort to work on his difficulties so long as he would not be forced to talk. During the intake session, he expressed pity for his father, pent-up anger toward his mother, and self-accusation and anger combined with a low self-image. That was the extent of the information he verbally conveyed regarding himself.

It should be mentioned that Jonas had never experienced music therapy, nor had he been exposed to music or to other artistic modalities, with the exception of visual arts. Subsequent to listening to his playing during the intake session, I noted and concluded the following:

> 1. Jonas (on the right side of the piano) played a duet with me (on the left side of the piano). Jonas had a virginal style, as he had never had formal piano lessons. He increased the volume, tempo, and intensity of the music as he limited his playing to the upper register of the keyboard. His piano playing was restricted, repetitive,[3] and fast. I supported him on the bass register, and the musical character he established was undoubtedly expressionistic.

> 2. Jonas beat the drum as I accompanied him on the piano. I again noted the rapid, animated tempo. The beating was not persistent, strong, or steady. It reminded me more of a pot that is about to boil over and burst. Indeed, when Jonas listened to a recording of the two passages, he commented: "I know I have a lot of pent-up wrath. I can hear it in my music. But I also hear that I cannot express intense emotion and I cannot cry."

Therapeutic Rationale

I perceived Jonas as a sad, angry, and confused young man. During the four years of his mother's illness, he lived with his family in crowded, intimate quarters. At the same time, he never conversed openly with the additional members of his family, since he was brought up in an inhibited atmosphere and his mother's illness had always been considered a deep secret. Jonas's impressions of his mother were extremely vivid. He described her in the following manner:

> [She was] domineering, harsh, oppressive. [She would] lie there in the room and let me irritate everyone. [She let me be] a nuisance and a troublemaker.

On the other hand, he described his father as helpless and passive. He had devoted himself to his work and had found it difficult to express feelings toward his children. I noticed that the musical activity gave Jonas a sense of comfort and detected a smile on his face when he engaged in the new experience of "speaking" through music. My assumption was that the musical expression in itself would suffice in the initial stages of therapy and that Jonas would benefit from experiencing music as an expressive language. Accordingly, in the first stages of therapy, my main goals were to help Jonas express himself, to allow him to develop trust in me, and to encourage him to employ music as a therapeutic language.

THERAPEUTIC PROCESS

Representations (first three months of music therapy)

Jonas used two instruments to carry on a conversation with his deceased mother. He chose a piano to represent his mother and a dulcimer to represent himself, "because I am weak and gentle and she is strong and domineering." In this musical dialogue, Jonas demonstrated his symbolic ability through his use of the instruments and particularly through his choice of the dulcimer to represent himself: He played gently but with confidence, showing that he had something to say. The dialogue was quite lengthy (30 minutes). After listening to the recording, Jonas made the following observation:

> I made a real effort to tell her how angry I am at her, how she stopped being a mother and stopped caring about her children, how long I have been angry at her, and how afraid I am to be angry at the dead.

The verbal elaboration of this material dealt with the difficulty of harboring ambivalent feelings (e.g., love-hate) toward one's mother, and how Jonas had suffered while his mother was ill and after she had died and his need to express those intense feelings, a need that he had still found difficult to satisfy.

In the following session, we replayed the musical dialogue and verbal summary. After listening again to the musical dialogue with his mother, Jonas jotted down the following comments:

> I tell you, Mother. I feel sad, but cannot cry. I feel angry, but cannot scream. I am rotten, but I cannot purify myself. I am doomed. I want to play to the end, to undo everything that has been distorted, to undo all those years of decay, hallucinations, escape. Let me be free. The piano is resolute, painful and violent. The string [of the dulcimer] is angry, wipes its tears away, and goes on. It is handsome, strong, determined and human.

This emotional material and the confrontation of his mother repeated themselves throughout several sessions with mild variations. As aforementioned, in this process of dealing with unfinished business between Jonas and his deceased mother, the piano represented his mother and the dulcimer represented Jonas himself. Jonas's comments (quoted above) gave me the impression that he had begun to see a new dawn.

Breathing and Vocality (fifth month of therapy)

The feeling of filth and decay that Jonas had verbally described and portrayed through music was so strong that I suggested he work on breathing. This suggestion was based on my knowledge of the profound changes such work can bring about in a person's physical state (which might generate changes in one's state of mind). Jonas accepted the idea, and we began working intensively on vocality and movement, which are usually elicited by breathing. The following poem was the product of exercises that focused on full diaphragm breathing combined with movement:

> The wind blows through the leaves
> and I am crying there in the rain.
> All I want is to lie on the cold sidewalk
> to let the drops mix with my tears and cry there,
> to flow with the water and scream at the top of my lungs,
> to let air into my body and be there with it.
> All of the excrement and rot is being washed to the sea,
> all of it is comes out until I turn yellowish-green.
> I stay there, squeezed out like a lemon,
> and I can start anew, I can start living like a human being.
> I just don't want the filth, that's all.
> I will cry to the end,
> I will strike a blow and don't care if I die from it.

The Process of Transition from One Artistic Modality to Another (seventh month of therapy)

At the beginning of the session, I intentionally played ecstatic music from the Atlas Mountains, which inspired Jonas to draw a self-portrait:

SELF-PORTRAIT

When he finished, he explained: "I drew myself and showed how all of my feelings are tearing my face apart." In relation to this, I would like to mention that the following was written in the manifesto of the expressionist *Die Brücke* movement: "Throw fire on the crust and make it molten, liquid, until its meaning emerges from the inside [core] and breaks through its grieving crust" (Javlensky, 1948).

This is the feeling that emerges when one looks at Jonas's self-portrait. I suggested that Jonas continue working on the portrait by vocalizing it. He did so while turning his back to me and placing the painting in front of him. He began with faint humming and built up to a scream. When the recording was replayed, Jonas commented: "I am singing about the naughty boy inside me. [I am singing] about how I hate you for bringing me into this world, about my social isolation, about the dirt that has stuck to me, about my desire to purify myself and be born again or else die."

The more Jonas began to trust me as his therapist, the more he began to express fatalistic thoughts and exhibit self-destructive tendencies. I was on guard, and when I sensed that Jonas was in danger, I sought counsel with a professional psychiatrist (in accordance with the code of professional ethics of the Israeli Association of Creative and Expressive Therapies).[4]

Guided Imagery in Music (GIM) (ninth month of therapy)

Jonas was very agitated upon his arrival at the session following a harsh and candid discussion with his father. His father had found it difficult to accept the things that Jonas had said to him. Jonas, however, felt that this was the first time he had actually told his father what he thought of him and his deceased mother and of the difficulty that he and his father had in communicating with each other. The father had become very frightened and asked to meet with me because he attributed the son's outburst to the therapeutic process. I requested Jonas's permission to meet with his father, and he expressed his consent through the following comment: "I will make everyone dirty so that I can finally cleanse myself."

My individual meeting with Jonas's father was extremely beneficial for all parties involved in the therapeutic process. I observed that his father was at a loss: He wanted to help his son but didn't know how. He was willing to participate in the therapy sessions with his son. Nonetheless, I explained to him that this would not be feasible and suggested that he seek separate psychotherapy. The father told me of the trauma the family had endured during the four years of his wife's illness and mentioned that this had been the first time he had discussed his feelings regarding it.

In the sessions with Jonas, the topic of death was constantly discussed. He confided that he had contemplated suicide about a year before his mother had died, but that the forces of life had prevailed. In his words: "Today I want to calm down, and I am asking you to help me do it." For this purpose, I chose guided imagery, which included breathing exercises to music (involving tension and relaxation movements). I chose a composition written by the Israeli poet Zelda just before her death, adapted by singer Adi Etzion and composer Yehoshua Ben-Yehoshua. The passage is intense and highly expressive. In this respect, it is completely different from the "New Age Music" or meditation passages commonly used by therapists today. This composition actually highly corresponded with Jonas's expressionistic creations. During the elaboration process following the listening phase, Jonas said:

> I saw a bird—a raven—flying against a background of mountains, rivers, and cliffs, perhaps like the view one sees from this window. And I heard birds chirping. The raven did not care about the other birds and preferred to be on his own: independent. I also saw a white dove looking down from the sky. She looked very strange, as though she were half-dead. Then, suddenly, the raven saw blood and understood that it was his own. At once I was there. I observed the scene from the side. Then the raven fell to the ground and I dug into the earth, into the blood and gore.

Jonas later arrived at the conclusion that he was the raven and that the blood was the filth he felt inside, while the white dove was the spirit of his deceased mother looking down on him and observing his every motion. I asked Jonas if he would like to actualize the dream in music and he consented. He chose the drum to represent himself (preferring a powerful instrument for himself for the first time), the dove was represented by an autoharp, and the landscape was represented by a variety of percussion instruments. At his request, I played the mother and the landscape, while he focused on expressing himself.

Childhood Memories

Jonas was very calm throughout the next session. He told me that he had done much contemplating during the week and that many childhood memories had revisited him. For example:

> My mother shut me in the house and made me sit in front of a glass of milk. "Don't move until you drink all of your milk" [she had said]. I sat there for hours and didn't drink a drop. My mother yelled at me [and said] that I was always dirty and she wiped me against my will. I remember when I was six years old and flew like a bird on the slopes to the school It was a real experience in flying. ... I hate milk, with something that smells like a turpentine or gasoline. I believed I was really dirty. In elementary school, I always felt I was abnormal, retarded, even though I always did my schoolwork well. I liked to play a kind of roulette: I burned weeds and even burned my room. Now I think I played the part of the bad, disturbed boy, a label I had been given by my family.

Jonas mentioned that these childhood recollections, which had escaped his memory for several years, had brought him relief and encouraged him to make decisions concerning his life. Since this session did not involve any musical activities, it took place in the area of the therapy room that was mainly reserved for verbal discussions. I would like to note that verbal communication, which Jonas had been so adamantly opposed to during the intake session, was an integral aspect of the therapeutic process, particularly during the phases of elaboration. The verbal communication was prompted by the experiential musical activities. Furthermore, if we carefully take note of his memories, it appears as though Jonas had already experienced problems in his childhood and that his mother's illness had simply been the spark that had set the bramble field on fire.

To Sing and Cry: Vocal Expressionism (one year of therapy)

There is nothing like the voice to reflect the emotional turmoil, pain, cracks, and venomous snakes inside us. Two examples from Jonas's vocal period were meaningful. Both were revealing and embarrassing and continued for over 15 minutes.

The first example is a vocal improvisation of a repetitive harmonic sequence provided by the music therapist:

C – Em – F – C / C – Em – F – E7 / Am – Em – F – C / Dm – D7 –G //

Jonas improvised freely without words on this "holding" frame. His improvisation began with a soft, timid voice and developed into a "sky-piercing cry." As a therapist, I found some of the moments in which I persisted with the harmonic frame extremely difficult in their expressionistic revelation. It was as though the patient were ripping open his stomach and revealing its contents. It should be mentioned that after maintaining the repetitive harmonic sequence for five minutes, I was able to develop the musical content and follow the dynamical changes imparted in Jonas's vocality. These musical changes and developments helped us endure the 15-minute process.

The second example is a vocal improvisation of his to which he gradually added words while the music therapist followed his voice and the words with the piano. I noted the change of registers in Jonas's voice, the free vocality and highly expressive text that recapitulated the motifs elicited in previous sessions: "I am walking over an abyss of fear … I am running … I am hitting … I am tearing … ."

A Lullaby of Conciliation (conclusion of therapy)

From this phase, I would like to bring an example of a conciliation that Jonas initiated. It was a vocal a cappella[5] improvisation in which Jonas very softly sang to his mother in a lullaby style. At a certain moment, he asked me to be the mother and join him in his singing. It thus became a duet in which each participant had an independent polyphonic role. Both from a musical point of view and in a psychological aspect, this improvisation was new and very touching and summarized a period.

SUMMARY

The process described above was not completed. Unfortunately, due to technical reasons we could not really conclude the course of therapy.

This case leaves off at the point where Jonas could openly express himself. His relationship with his father had improved considerably. At the same time, he had wrapped up some of his "unfinished business" with his mother to the point where he was able to continue working on some of the emotionally loaded issues more maturely than before. In terms of practical-rehabilitative outcomes, he had changed his lifestyle and made a brave decision to leave home, where he had been stifled in many ways. This presented him with the opportunity to cope with the real world, which had frightened him so terribly in the past.

As I see it, the main contribution of music therapy was to enable Jonas to express himself through "primary communication" (Noy, 1999, chapter 1), a language that touched the bare roots of his soul long before he could employ verbal expression and gain better insight. Nevertheless, verbal elaboration was an essential aspect of therapy that was accomplished in different ways: through face-to-face conversation, verbal associations elicited by music, poetry writing, and translation of his own musical creations into words and vice versa.

Notes

(1) Reuven Morgan was born in Wales, became a renowned actor and theater director, and performed in the Shakespearean theater in England. He emigrated to Israel in the early sixties and worked for Israeli Broadcasting (Kol Israel). Morgan was the first teacher of the drama school of the radio, directing programs, translating, writing, narrating English literature, and more. Reuven Morgan invested many hours in my 1996 book, *Music: Motion and Emotion,* of which he translated three chapters. He died of cancer a few months later and was buried in the Christian Cemetery in the German Colony in Jerusalem. I dedicate this chapter to Reuven Morgan, who illuminated my world with his theatrical and linguistic knowledge.

(2) Borderline Personality Disorder: "A personality disorder characterized by a pervasive pattern of impulsivity and unstable personal relationship, self-image, and affect. Beginning in early childhood ..." (Colman, 2001, p. 99).

(3) Repetitive style in music has varied meaning. It might symbolize avoidance of free expression due to deep anxiety and low self-esteem.

Repetitions may thereby function as a calming defense mechanism and, when employed by the therapist, may serve as a holding and containing frame (see also Sekeles, 1996, p. 37).

(4) ICET, The Israeli Association of Creative and Expressive Therapies, is an umbrella association to all art therapies in Israel (dance and movement, music, visual arts, drama, psychodrama and bibliotherapy). Established in 1971, it has three branches and holds yearly study days, seminars, workshops, and conferences.

(5) A cappella means singing without instrumental accompaniment: a pure vocal performance. In the aforementioned case, it developed into two melodic lines sung in a counterpoint style, symbolizing the child Jonas and his deceased mother.

Chapter Nine

EDWIN, WHO MURDERED HIS WIFE

IN A PSYCHOTIC ATTACK

A CASE ANALYSIS

"Set me as a seal upon thine heart, as a seal upon thine arm;
for love is strong as death; jealousy is cruel as the grave;
the coals thereof are coals of fire,
which hath a most vehement flame."
("Solomon's Song," chapter 8:6)

INTRODUCTION

Edwin was a tall, handsome man in his late twenties when he was hospitalized in the psychiatric hospital in which I was employed. He referred himself to music therapy, presenting himself as a folk musician who could not live without music. After obtaining confirmation from his psychiatrist, I began to work with him simultaneously in both individual and group therapy. The process endured five years of ups and downs, regressions and progressions, deep depressions, and periods of flourishing creativity. Edwin had been a stranger in this particular country as I myself had been. We were both faced to cope with being immigrants; we both came from different language and musical cultures and had to contend with a new mentality as well as with the cultural gap between client and therapist.

Individual Intake

INTRODUCTION. Edwin was diagnosed as suffering from schizo-affective disorder in which there are clinical symptoms present from both categories of schizophrenia and affective diseases. Edwin exhibited pathological signs in his early adulthood. He married when he was 19 years old, and his wife bore a baby daughter a year later. By that time, his condition had deteriorated. He was hospitalized and released home two years afterward. His relationship with his wife had been a complicated one from the very beginning: A cultural gap had existed between them, she hadn't been able to cope with his illness and occasional aggressive outbursts, and he had always been suspicious of her and had a preset misgiving concerning the origin of his daughter. Schizo-affective disorder has schizo-depressive waves and schizo-manic waves. During one of the schizo-manic waves, Edwin had killed his wife with his own two hands, handed the baby over to a neighbor, and hospitalized himself. When I first met Edwin, he had already been hospitalized for a year (second hospitalization).[1]

The music therapy room was very spacey, furnished with ancient furniture. It had tall, narrow windows; a stony floor; a cage with midget parrots; and some flourishing plants. Musical instruments hung from the walls; huge, self-made pottery drums and an upright piano covered the floor; and ancient records and big cassettes sat on bookshelves. The room was an antithesis of a traditional hospital space and enabled both individual and group music therapy. In addition, I was technically able to build musical instruments there with the patients, thereby developing creativity as well as saving on budget expenses.[2]

PROCESS. When Edwin first entered the room, he immediately chose the guitar and began to play and sing a spiritual piece. He sang in English and continued, moving from one song to the other. Half an hour passed as Edwin played. I listened and no word was uttered. In the meantime, the sun sank, the room darkened, and Edwin had to return to his ward. As he left, he said: "Next time, I'll play my own composed songs."

Throughout the entire session, he had not expressed interest in the various possibilities the music room offered and had attempted only what he had felt comfortable with, singing and accompanying himself. His playing had been clear and fluent, his bass voice warm and beautiful, and it had been apparent to me that he possessed natural talent. His mood had been somewhat quiet and reserved.

Group Intake

INTRODUCTION. The group was composed of three patients hospitalized from 20 to 35 years, plus Edwin. They were all from the same ward. The condition of the additional three group members was that of chronic patients. This was at a time when the psychotropic treatment (psychiatric drugs) was at an early stage of development, in comparison to the present. The three members of the group, Anton, David, and Donald, were diagnosed as schizophrenic patients. They were very passive, barely spoke, and expressed themselves through a kind of muttering-speech and sometimes through neologism.[3] They moved about mechanically and suffered from uncontrolled movements and salivation, hallucinations, and disorders of thought, affect, and perception. Anton and Donald were especially paranoid[4] and were certain that they were being eavesdropped on through the radio's wires and that the FBI was after them. They all experienced side effects[5]; David entered a catatonic state[6] several times and most of the time seemed to be "out of reach."

All members of the group participated in both individual and group music therapy. In addition, due to a tradition I had regulated at this hospital, they also contributed once a month to an open evening, in which music was presented and created in a free fashion. Patients (sometimes 100) and staff members participated in these evenings. This tradition helped us to make music a welcome guest at our hospital and easily celebrate holidays and other festivities. My view was that most of our patients considered the hospital their home. We therefore needed to integrate musical activities to enrich the entire community and not just those who participated in the music therapy sessions. For the open evenings, we occasionally invited well-known performers or music students and at times attended concerts outside the hospital or took musical instruments to play-sing in nature.

From this short description, it is probably clear that the patients attending the small therapy group knew each other from other activities, had individual music therapy sessions, and were willing to take part in group music therapy. Consequently, the intake-observation session was as natural a process as possible for them.

INITIATIVES. Edwin took the guitar, asked the others to choose musical instruments, and formed an improvisational group. The patients were obviously pleased that Edwin had taken the initiative and responsibility. Edwin played a South American rhythmical tune and the others joined in with drums, sticks, and rattles. As they were familiar with recordings, with their permission we recorded the group improvisation and listened to it afterward. Although Edwin was the initiator, the leader, and the domineering figure throughout the improvisation, at the end of the session he himself suggested that next time they decide together what to do. In his next individual session, he said to me: "I apologize for assuming your role, but I know those people have no energy and I wanted to help you." In the short conversation that ensued, I told him that his idea of sharing would be very helpful and encouraging for the entire group. A week later, it was obvious that Edwin was entering a schizo-manic wave. His mood became heightened; he began to speak of his talents in an exaggerated manner, had some paranoid thoughts, and sometimes lost control. It was easier to handle him in individual music therapy than within the group.

From here on, after describing the music therapy settings in which Edwin participated, I would like to focus mainly on Edwin's development as a result of both group music therapy and the individual sessions.

When Edwin brought his own composed songs to therapy, I took note of several issues:

- Edwin's last song had been composed five years ago.
- The themes of his writing were nature, love, and, generally, sweet, "chocolate box" content.
- He could write songs in two languages but preferred English.
- Edwin communicated through his songs but remained in the safe land of poetic beauty.
- Even when he wrote a love song, he generalized it and did not touch upon his personal feelings.
- Most of his songs had probably been written during schizo-manic phases.

Therapeutic Considerations

The group was based on the ward psychiatrist's recommendation. Edwin was much less regressed than the other members of the group. In a way, this position contributed to his self-confidence, specifically due to his authentic talent and development in music. Through music, he was able to experience himself as strong, creative, and contributing. Paradoxically, this also created a problem that hadn't existed in individual therapy, as he threatened the group members' already limited ability to take initiative. This led them to become even more passive and to delegate the responsibility of action to Edwin. On the other hand, Edwin supplied the group with a natural leader, which Freud (1921) declared an essential condition of group therapy. Moreover, this provided an opportunity for constructive work within the group on sharing, cooperation, and mutual creation rather than eventually allowing the members of the group to reject Edwin. I therefore planned to develop and maintain several organizational conditions concerning the group:

- Set rules to enable continuity.
- Establish group tradition.
- Encourage individual development and functioning.
- Shift leadership.
- Build a supportive group.
- Get the group to contribute to the hospital's community life.

As all members of the group participated in individual music therapy, I supposed that in this setting it would be possible to accentuate the work on weaker functions in favor of the group therapy.

As aforementioned, Edwin had stated that he would try to be less domineering in the group, and I had to wait to see if he would indeed keep his word. In reality, he became less and less dominant and much more sociable.

Approach and Technique

1. Warm-up (Movement)

Throughout the years I worked as a music therapist with psychiatric patients, I always took care to invest the beginning of each session in preparing for whatever came afterward ("warming up," as employed in the terminology of dance-movement therapists). Indeed, this mostly included body-movement work, either active or receptive. With chronic patients, I found that receptive-meditative exercises may attain a negative result by intensifying the patient's isolation and regression. I thereby employed mostly energetic movement techniques with gradual deceleration. These included guided movements (guided by music and by the therapist's instruction) or improvisations stimulated by the music alone. Repeating these every session contributed to the continuity as well as to the establishment of traditional customs in the group.

Chronic psychiatric patients require many repetitions and safe boundaries to strengthen their poor self-confidence and enable the development of trust both in the therapist and in the members of the group. In a way, this group often behaved as children, which makes it appropriate to quote Slavson's (1952) words:

> In individual therapy, the client relates himself to the therapist; in group therapy, the intent is that the child should relate himself to the group as well as to the individuals in it. The therapist's role is that of catalytic agent in this process. His attitude of acceptance, friendliness, and appreciativeness sets up like attitudes in the children toward one another. The group therapist is also a synthesizing influence for the group (p. 138).

The opening of each session soon produced positive results: Those patients who were very passive most of the day became more energetic and began to use their bodies in new ways. Edwin, who came from a culture that encouraged movement, had a natural way with movement and undoubtedly inspired the others. This introduction would last 15 minutes and was divided into instructed and free movement.

2. The Musical Circle

The following stage consisted of sitting in a circle and, after a short discussion and a mutual decision, making music. As for the verbal part, generally speaking it had been very poor. Many times, I felt that they had simply forgotten how to talk. Conversely, knowing that I was a foreigner to their language, they amazed me by trying extra hard to be clear. Edwin's speech, on the other hand, was clear, but he lacked the desire to verbally share any content with the group. In his individual music therapy, I had the chance to work on this very issue.

3. Folk Songs and Singing

After the abovementioned segment of the group therapy, we moved to closing the hour. This was done by singing the members' ethnical songs according to their choice. At first, they preferred to leave the choice to me, but it gradually became apparent to them that the hour was theirs and so was the responsibility. I decided to place books with folk music and texts in the center of our circle and to allow the patients to choose. Each chosen song was typed up afterward, allowing us to later form a book from the songs we collected over the years. The members of the group (including Edwin) chose songs from their childhood and adolescence. Those songs reminded them of a better era in their life and aroused nostalgic feelings.

As music therapists, when we work abroad in a different musical culture, it is imperative to study the new culture and mentality and to attempt to understand and imagine its importance for the local residents or, in this case, for the patients. I would sit for endless hours learning entire song books, preparing myself for my patients' requests. I believed, among other things, that it gave the patients a sense of "being honored." Edwin added a colorful mood to the folk songs by bringing songs from his childhood and country and teaching us a few. Eventually, David said to me: "Bring songs from the Holy Land." This request was very moving from a man who barely spoke. I indeed added a couple of Israeli songs to their collection that I translated to enable the group to sing them.[7]

The voice is the most natural musical instrument, the one we carry with us everywhere. Singing integrates physical operation (the use of organs that participate in this action: throat, vocal cords, diaphragm, lungs) with emotional expression by employing the natural musical elements that create emotionality: range of voice, volume, and tempo; socialization (togetherness, sharing, creating varied interactions, and group cohesion); and cognitive skills (the use of language).

Randi Rolvsjord (2005), who wrote from her experience in psychiatry, listed the following features: Songs are a common form of expression; songs can be performed over and over again; songs can be shared; songs can be kept and stored away (p. 98).

The singing of folk songs and the growing interest in facilitating the voice brought about a new development in the group.

4. Composing Personal Songs

Edwin brought his previously composed songs to his individual sessions and gradually began to work on new material. Though he touched upon more emotional issues through them, he never mentioned the circumstances that led him to murder his wife. Neither was this topic brought up by the other patients. The psychiatrist of the ward, who was also my supervisor, advised me not to touch on the subject unless Edwin elicited it. In the meantime, Edwin's songs began to emit a sad, tragic color: They described loneliness, hostility, disappointment, failure in relationships with women, and a feeling of not being understood. I sensed that this circumventing approach was his way of sharing personal material and of grieving for his wife and his son.

At times, he would bring a song he composed to a group session and perform it. Once, Anton suddenly suggested writing a group hymn. Working on this hymn, a new gate was opened in which words began to play an important role. This held true for all the members of the group.

Another phenomenon was that because Edwin and I had not yet mastered the language, the three schizophrenic patients took on a more active role. They would also at times introduce neologism, to which I agreed on the condition that the one responsible would explain the meaning of the word to the group. We performed this exercise by writing on a large board so that everyone would be able to contribute a word, an idea, a sentence, etc. We would discuss the content and try to agree on it. I was very pleased to witness the patients arguing over a word or an idea and to watch them emerge from their shells. Edwin became very active and was actually happy to learn the language, as in individual music therapy he wrote only in English. In order to stimulate and encourage the members to participate in the writing, I used word games, nonsense sentences, descriptive sentences, word or sentence completion, the choosing of keywords, etc. (see Wigram, 2005, pp. 246–265).

Composing the music was sometimes done after the text was prepared and at other times preceded the text. I assisted by accompanying the creation of the melody on the piano through different techniques, such as allowing each patient to improvise on one sentence and working on it until it became integrated in the song. It often took three weeks or more to finish a song, gradually becoming the project of our second book.

5. The Creation of a Musical

Edwin came up with the idea of composing a musical on the everyday life of the psychiatric patient and the manner in which the normal community perceived him/her. This idea frightened Anton, David, and Donald, but Edwin convinced them and so the work began.

Brainstorming and Creation

This stage lasted one month, during which we gathered topics of interest so that all members of the group would be able to participate and contribute. As in group composing, I used the school board in a way that required the participants to raise their heads, an act that is difficult for someone pumped up with medication and fatigued part of the time. These were the topics elicited by the group in their chronological order:

> Our pills.
> The nurses.
> The psychiatrist.
> Good morning, how are you today?
> Potatoes-animals on the plate.
> We want to get out, to be free.
> We're home?
> I wish I could stay in bed.
> I wish I would die.
> I feel lonely.
> My wife left me and took the children.
> I killed my wife and lost my son.
> I feel depressed.
> We are strange.
> We frighten people and they hate us.

From this list, which was accompanied by slow, tiresome discussions, we were able to learn a lot about the patients: They were concerned with the enduring necessity to swallow pills, and, in the conversations, all four expressed the fear that the pills were poisoning them and that the nurses and doctors wanted to get rid of them. They also admitted that they sometimes threw the pills away.

Indeed, a severe problem of compliance exists concerning psychotropic medicine. This was specifically the case at the beginning stages of psychotropic development. Many patients resisted, were afraid of the side effects, did not understand the correlation between the medication and its influence, held prejudiced notions regarding the subject, etc. Elizur, Tyano, Munitz, and Neumann (1990) claim that compliance consists of physiological, pharmacological, and psychological aspects that are of cardinal importance in psychiatry (p. 397). Understandably, the fact that the patients had permitted themselves to open up and discuss this issue had already provided them with a sense of relief. In addition, I invited their psychiatrist to one of our group sessions to broaden the discussion and moderate the anxiety.

The song composed on the pills dealt with all of the aspects they had mentioned during the brainstorming, with Edwin serving as the main originator of the melody.

Another subject was the nurses and psychiatrists (the medical team). The patients felt as though they acted as jail wardens, although I must say objectively that it was one of the most advanced and enlightened hospitals I have ever observed. This had, however, been their subjective feeling, and at that stage I had to contain it.

Anton said that every morning when the nurse asked him, "How are you today, Anton?," he envisioned her as an inquisitor who wanted to harm him. Sometimes she looked like a black queen with long nails to him. Donald, who also had strong paranoid traits, said that he couldn't stand certain foods because they turned to animals, beasts, or insects on his plate. This instigated a lengthy conversation on the misery of hallucinations and delusions, issues they mainly dealt with through denial. The second song that was created described the way they perceived the medical team and how they experienced the world. The music was gradually composed by all members of the group, with my harmonic support on the piano.

Following these occurrences, they embarked on a phase in which they began to discuss their isolation and loneliness. Then, suddenly, Edwin raised his issue: "I killed my wife and lost my son." It seemed as though the members of the group accepted this statement with no wonder or fear, as though they had previously discussed it. I knew from the psychiatrist that they all knew, but that Edwin had never mentioned his history. We agreed to work on it in individual music therapy, but this never transpired. Edwin raised the topic and closed it in the same breath. It did, however, prompt him to talk about his loneliness, sadness, and anxieties.

The last subjects, "We are strange," "We frighten people and they hate us," were easier for the group to deal with, as they tended to split their reality into them/the world and we/the inside prisoners. It was amazing how incredibly overloaded their emotional world was and that they were able to work on such topics though they were severely chronic patients, hospitalized for 20 or more years. Throughout this entire lengthy process, Edwin served as a member who could clarify what others had stammered or had muttered inaudibly with a few words. It was obvious that he gained much self-confidence from this process. My objective as therapist was to provide each participant a place of respect among the group members although their contributions were different or unequal.

The musical was never completed. The group composed six songs in over half a year, but from my point of view, it was a great achievement mainly due to the process they had undergone and, in a way, also due to the results they obtained.

I would like to take this opportunity to point out the importance of "end products" as well as of the "therapeutic process," in light of the fact that as therapists we ought to not only work toward a psychodynamic objective but also strive toward rehabilitation as well. Even within the framework of a hospital, it is essential to pay our respects to the therapeutic products and to share them with the community.

I have often heard therapists claim that the most important objective in therapy is the process, while the by-products or end products are secondary and less important. I completely disagree with this notion and believe that anyone who has ever witnessed a patient's delight when listening to his recorded song and transcribed music would agree with me.

The process is the road and the gate through which evolution and development bear a product. This gives the patient something to hold on to. Indeed, one of the strongest attributes of the art therapies is the opportunity they proffer to relisten to, reobserve, and reread the artistic creativity and thus to sense an increased productivity and normalcy.

EPILOGUE

This was a chapter on Edwin, but also on group therapy with chronic patients in psychiatric hospitalization. In order to understand Edwin, it was necessary to follow his development in both individual music therapy and in group music therapy. Individual music therapy provided him with the opportunity to further develop his natural creative talents, to progress from composing beautiful songs dealing with love and nature (while denying his tormented disposition) to more personal material dealing with grief and sadness. The group music therapy allowed him to feel part of a small community and to contribute to chronic-passive members and taught him to maintain modesty in order to gain friendship and acceptance. He not only gained the respect of the group members but also encouraged their involvement and even their speech. Irving Yalom (1985) wrote, concerning group therapy: "The greater the verbal participation, the greater the sense of involvement and the more the patient is valued by the others and ultimately by himself" (p. 385). In a group of chronic psychiatric patients, where each word was worth gold, this importance was doubled.

We never succeeded in working in depth with Edwin on the murder of his wife, but he did work on it in an indirect manner by expressing his mood, grief, and loneliness. He participated in concerts, gained much acknowledgment on the ward, and was released after six years of hospitalization to a sheltered housing complex in the community. Ten years afterward, I was informed that he had undergone a severe crisis and hanged himself.

This was the last song he wrote in therapy (translated). It was written in a blues musical style:

> I am a deserter from birth
> Deserted my country
> Deserted my family
> Deserted my son.
> I am an eternal orphan
> I am a father of an orphan

We are both orphans
Lonely in our caves.
Murdered in our caves.

Notes

(1) Schizophrenic patients are usually nonviolent. Statistically, there are fewer violent occurrences among schizophrenics than in the general population. On the other hand, there is a greater chance for short life expectancy due to the danger of suicidal tendencies (Elizur et al., 1990).

(2) The personal building of musical instruments is an activity that suits long-term hospitalized patients. In psychiatric hospitals, there are gardens kept partly by the patients. This provides the opportunity to plant gourds and other seeds, to observe their growth, and to then prepare a personal musical instrument. The therapist can consequently offer musical instruments made both of natural material and of metal, plastic, and junk material with personal designs. Besides the creative act and the patients' pleasure, there is a great economical advantage to this activity, provided that the musical instrument is strong and of good quality.

(3) Neologism is a typical phenomenon among schizophrenic patients that depicts the formation of sentences and words with personal meaning, incomprehensible by the listener (Dorland, 1982).

(4) Paranoid schizophrenia is the most common type of schizophrenia. The general organization of the personality is higher than in other types. It is characterized by the presence of delusional thoughts of persecution, jealousy, and grandeur. The patient is tense, suspicious of the environment, hostile, and occasionally violent (Dorland, 1982).

(5) The side effect of psychotropic drugs is an adverse reaction. It might appear in the form of sedation, dystonia, extrapyramidal phenomena, and others.

(6) Catatonia in schizophrenia may present a psychiatric emergency in the stage of either stupor or excitement. With the new generation of psychotropic drugs, these phenomena are less readily observed (World

Health Organization, 1996).

(7) The cultural issue in therapy and in music therapy is a very important one. I live in a country that has absorbed immigrants from all around the world, in which the "melting pot" became an idiom of negative as well as positive content. It was never enough to study the musical culture of your patients or music therapy students; it really required you to take a thorough look into the cultural mentality: language, history, customs, beliefs, etc. The folk song is just one example, though very important in our profession. In a symposium on the cultural background of the therapist and the patient, I once heard a prominent music therapist state: "If those immigrants came to my country out of their own free will, they must attempt to understand us and assimilate into the new mentality." I completely disagree: We as therapists should assume upon ourselves the responsibility of encouraging new immigrants to cope with the new reality, partly by studying the patient's old reality and demonstrating respect for it, rather than attempt to erase his or her past. From this point of view, the group had fulfilled Edwin's need to be respected through the mutual sharing of culture.

Chapter Ten

THE GRIEF OF THE THERAPIST OVER PATIENTS WHO PASSED AWAY

"Do not boast thyself of tomorrow;
for thou knowst not what a day may bring forth"
(Proverbs 27:1)

Dedicated to the music therapy patients who passed away

INTRODUCTION

I discussed the content of this chapter with students and colleagues at length. As a result, I decided to conclude my book in a personal manner, based on my own experience in the field of music therapy.

Most music therapists have lost patients during the course of their clinical work: sometimes during the therapeutic process; sometimes, as in the case of a terminal patient, at the expected termination of therapy (Nathaniel, chapter 3); or sometimes years after therapy has ended (Avi: car accident, chapter 7; Edwin: suicide, chapter 9).

Many of my music therapy students at The David Yellin College in Jerusalem completed their internships in institutions where death was a common phenomenon and had to cope with the loss. Individual and group supervision may help in such cases, and, indeed, it is important to invest time and effort in dealing with loss during the course of studies. Every so often, a student would return from an internship and tell us that no one had bothered to inform him of the death of a patient. He would find himself standing in front of an empty bed, not knowing what to do. In other cases, the name of the patient (mostly with children) would not be erased from the activities board for months, with the topic not even being discussed with the other children. When a child disappears in an institute of severely sick children, it may cause more severe anxiety than when honest information is provided in a manner suitable to the child's cognitive and emotional level of development.

Students would raise questions such as, Should I attend the funeral? Should I visit the family during the Shiva (the first seven days of mourning in Judaism)? Such questions open the gate to important discussions regarding the therapist-patient relationship; emotions that arise with the death of a patient; the difference between therapy in an institution and therapy in a private setting; and what is to be done with the emotions? What are these emotions? Are they simply sadness, or are they also pain and insult relating to the therapeutic investment and the facing of loss? As far as I have observed, these and other questions concern not only students but also each of us music therapists when losing a patient. It took me ten years to collect the raw material for this book, analyze it, review the recordings, and more. This lengthy period was necessary given that it deals with the enigma of death and the loss suffered by the patients, but also because it brought me back time and again to my personal experiences of losing patients as well as to the cardinal question of what the differences are between the loss of a patient and the loss of a family member or a dear friend. I am not certain I have the right answers, but since this matter deals with varied professional and personal issues, I would like to at least explore it within my own limitations.

Grief

The general definition of grief is the internal response to loss: what we feel, what we think, what we imagine; the meaning we ascribe to the loss and the time we require to work through it. The grievance period is a time that might include sleep and appetite disturbances, concentration problems, difficulties with decision-making, loss of interest in things we once enjoyed, social withdrawal, confusion, and disorientation. And, as Ruth Bright (2002) writes, it is more than sadness: "It can include anger, humiliation, feelings of depression, disbelief, relief of tension ..." (p. vi).

Experience teaches us that when death is expected, as in terminal illnesses, and there is enough time for emotional departure, the process takes on more of a sense of closure, sometimes even of relief, knowing that the deceased will not longer have to endure pain and suffering. While this doesn't eliminate the pain and sadness, the egocentric part of loss (I was left alone, I suffer, why me?) is marginalized.

Nathaniel had passed away following a few months of intensive music therapy sessions. I had never met him before, I did not know him in depth from his past, and I was not a member of his family. I knew that he was dying and that I had to do my best to facilitate the most I could through the sessions. I had time to think about the end of the process, which motivated me to dedicate as much time, professionalism, and emotional attention as I possibly could to the course of therapy. When Nathaniel passed away, I felt sad, empty, and at the same time relieved for him that his agony was finally over. I attended the funeral with no psychological hesitation, knowing the practical and symbolic importance of the closing of the tombstone on the grave ("stimat golal": according to the ancient Jewish custom of rolling a round stone on the entrance of the burial cave), which does not leave death's irreversibility ambiguous. The Halacha (traditional Jewish laws) concerning burial do not attempt to beautify death. The deceased is buried and not hidden in a coffin so that his body will come in direct contact with the earth, as it is instructed in the Bible: *"From dust thou art, and unto dust shalt thou return"* (Genesis 3:19).

While the physical aspect of death has a precise timing, the emotional departure has no date or precise place. This is why whenever we encounter death along our paths, it connects us to the process of mourning.

Mourning

Mourning takes the internal grief and expresses it externally: visitations of the family, the funeral, visiting the cemetery, memorial days, erecting the grave-tomb, different customs, and more. Its objective is to assist the development of a new relationship with the departed based on memory and the reconstruction of meaning in life. The process of grieving eventually reaches an end, but the process of mourning may be very long. Eliyahu Rosenheim (2003) describes grief and mourning as a "passage-ritual" that guides the bereaved person in how to cope with death and adjust to life without the deceased (p. 174). Rosenheim claims that from a psychological point of view, the irreversibility of death enables the shift to the next phase, which Freud defines as "work of mourning" (p. 199). This term describes the intrapsychic process whereby the bereaved person gradually manages to detach himself from the object (Freud, 1917).

How does this process relate to the therapist who has lost a patient? Once again, the process differs when we deal with a sudden death during or at the end of therapy in comparison to a death occurring years after therapy has ended. When Jacob's family asked me to bring his recorded music to the 30th-day ritual, I could hardly bring myself to do it. It took me a year to summarize his music therapy process (Sekeles, 1996, chapter 5). Jacob had died unexpectedly from a heart attack following two years of left hemiplegia due to a CVA (stroke). He had worked very hard on his damaged functions, had plans for the future, and managed very well with his deficiencies. We had both felt satisfaction and efficiency in regard to the process he had undergone. All of this had been cut short a few days following the termination of therapy. My immediate reaction after hearing the news was one of deep sadness mixed with anger and disappointment. I could scarcely accept the idea that the realization of so much work and mental investment had been taken within one minute by death. Of course, I could have assumed a different position, telling myself, for example, "Jacob invested his last two years in a productive way, proving his mental capacity and personal strength to his family, congregation, and himself. He died a sudden death and did not suffer," but at that moment, the personal "insult" had been too strong and I had to collect myself in order to gain a better emotional and cognitive angle. How did I work through it? To begin with, at that time I partook of psychoanalytically oriented supervision that enabled me to share my grief, mourning, and bereavement. The conversations with the supervisor were very important and gave me the energy to prepare the closure.

Preparing a Closure

1. Participating in the funeral and preparing musical material for the 30th-day memorial. This was done following the clear request of the deceased's wife and consultation with the supervisor with whom I worked at that time.
2. Writing a letter to the patient's wife and family. I took this initiative in light of the long cooperation and acquaintance I had had with his wife.
3. The following components are routinely completed

subsequent to the conclusion of a music therapy process, but in the case of death they also assist with emotional closure:

    a. Summarizing all the reports written after every session into one document.

    b. Summarizing the recordings, highlighting the most important moments in the patient's development.

4. Transcribing parts of the patient's improvised music and safeguarding them in his file.

5. Many years later: writing a case analysis as a chapter in my 1996 book.

All this served to create an emblem of the man or, in a way, a "working memorial monument."

Paying Respect by Playing

John had been suffering from early dementia due to severe alcoholism. In the past, he had been a well-known pianist-performer, but had lost his technical ability, memory, and dynamic performance skills. I worked with him through improvisations, a field he had not been fond of in his professional days, and through employing different techniques had gradually enabled him to return to playing short compositions. Yet again, this had been a mutual effort that bore mild fruits. Years later, I was informed of his death. In this case, I had to find an alternative way of paying my respect to John's memory. I did so by working on Chopin's *Revolutionary Étude,* ever so beloved by John, who had attempted to reconstruct it in his memory and fingers in spite of the agony he endured while doing so.

    As with the abovementioned points (3, 4, 5), this was an action taken by me alone, thus not interfering with possible ethical restrictions.

Suicide

Eric (a schizophrenic patient with whom I worked for four years, accompanying him through the thorny road from mutism to creativity) committed suicide many years after his release from the hospital, as had Edwin. Again, I had heard of the tragedy after I had left the hospital and returned to my homeland. Eric used to write to me from time to time, and consequently his death by suicide did not come as a real surprise to me. I had always harbored concern regarding his loneliness and desperation. Eric had persevered 20 years after leaving the hospital, but then had regressed and been hospitalized. In his final letter to me, he wrote: "I have the feeling that my music has been finished and that my life is back to zero" (Sekeles, 2005b). Edwin had also endured the world beyond the hospital for over ten years. With both, I had experienced a sense of deep desperation, of sitting far away, helpless, powerless to help. I knew that this did not reflect the actual reality and that these schizophrenic patients survived outside the hospital, but had many regressions and periods of hospitalization. I knew that they obtained very good treatment; however, emotionally, I still felt a responsibility. This is probably due to the long therapeutic alliance, the emotional investment, the idea of helping a very ill individual grow and develop within the boundaries of his condition, the closure of a long therapeutic process, and the disadvantage of geographic distance.

In his book *Suicide—The Tragedy of Hopelessness,* David Aldridge (1998) states:

> By concentrating on repeated sequences of interaction, the episode of suicidal behaviour can be constructed not as impulsive but as belonging within an extended time frame. Rather than punctuate reality into a short arc of critical disturbance, it is possible to see the episode as belonging to a cyclic pattern of escalating interaction (p. 276).

> For the person who is suicidal, then, distress has escalated beyond the threshold of their toleration. They have no more resources to sustain themselves. This is a process of desertification (p. 278).

Eric and Edwin had both been very lonely men: Edwin's wife had been killed by him, while Eric's had divorced him. Eric filled the emptiness with a musical group he organized with colleagues-patients; Edwin created some music but was not involved in any meaningful activity that might advance his contact with other human beings. It seemed as though they had indeed reached the threshold of their toleration.

Transforming the Energy of Grief

One of the ways that people cope with their grief and turn it into a positive, creative action is through a memorial gesture. For example:

- Choosing a special tombstone.
- Composing music.
- Organizing a musical evening.
- Arranging an album with photos.
- Publishing a book with the letters, poetry, etc., of the deceased.
- Making a film.
- Erecting a sculpture as a memorial monument.
- Cultivating a garden.

Some of these undertakings may help us as therapists, specifically when they incorporate music and do not interfere with the bereavement of the deceased's close family and friends. It is essential to remember that a therapist is not a member of the family and that interference beyond the empathic space might generate ethical problems. What the boundaries of this "empathic space" are depend in a way on individual therapeutic ideology. I know of therapists who would never attend the funeral of a patient and remain distanced even in the case of a child. Others are more flexible or even devoid of any boundaries. I prefer to maintain individual consideration and base my decisions according to each particular case that arises, i.e., to remain flexible within the ethical boundaries. Some ethical regulations are very clear concerning the appropriate behavior for a therapist in the incidence of a patient's death. For example, the Israeli association of clinical psychologists treats the ethical regulations for a deceased patient in the same way as it handles the regulations for a living patient. Conversely, the Israeli Association of Creative and Expressive Therapies does not broach the issue at all. Jehudit Achmon (2004, chapter 8) deals with the dual relationship in a very thorough book on *Ethical Issues for Professionals in Counseling and Psychotherapy*. In regard to writing about the patient, Achmon warns the therapist to be aware of and clear about his or her own interests, which may conflict with the patient's well-being (p. 174). Nonetheless, any contemplated action must first be discussed with the family members involved in order to obtain their consent.

It should be noted that Achmon's chapter discusses the relationship between two living people, the patient and the therapist, whereas what I'm concerned with in this last chapter is the reaction of the therapist following the death of his client. Obviously, when a patient's home is a hospital or other institution, as is most often the case with chronic patients, it might be healthier for the patients and the therapists to find a way to commemorate the deceased within the patient's community. When the setting is different, considerations should be made with regard to the specific situation, within the professional and personal ethical boundaries.

As rendered in this book, each chapter was dedicated to a deceased individual who influenced my personal and professional life. The last two chapters were dedicated to patients who passed away.

Death may be irreversible, but what we carry in our hearts and memories, the experiences we had with the deceased person, whether a family member, a friend, or a patient, accompany us for the rest of our lives and give meaning to our existence.

References

Achmon, J. (2004). Dual relationship. In G. Shefler, J. Achmon, & G. Weil (Eds.), *Ethical issues for professionals in counseling and psychotherapy* (pp. 160–178). Jerusalem: The Hebrew University, Magnes Press (Hebrew).

Aldridge, D. (1998a). *Suicide—The tragedy of hopelessness*. London: Jessica Kingsley Publishers.

Aldridge, D. (Ed.). (1998b). *Music therapy in palliative care*. London: Jessica Kingsley Publishers.

Amichai, Y. (1983). *The hour of mercy*. Tel Aviv: Schocken Publishing House (Hebrew).

Amichai, Y. (1985). *From man you are and to man you return*. Tel Aviv: Schocken Publishing House (Hebrew).

Amichai, Y. (1996). *The selected poetry of Yehuda Amichai*. Edited and translated by C. Bloch and S. Mitchell. Berkeley, CA: University of California Press.

Amir, D. (1998). The use of Israeli folk songs in dealing with women's bereavement and loss in music therapy. In D. Dokter (Ed.), *Arts therapists, refugees and migrants. Reaching across borders* (pp. 217–235). London: Jessica Kingsley Publishers.

Anastasiow, N. J. (1985). Parent training as adult development In S. Harel & N. J. Anastasiow (Eds.), *The at-risk infant: Psycho/socio/medical aspects* (pp. 75–85). London: Brooks.

Anderson, M., Tunaley, J., & Walker, J. (2000). *Relatively speaking: Communication in families*. Newcastle: University of Newcastle's Family Studies Centre.

Austin, W. W. (1966). *Music in the 20th century. From Debussy to Stravinsky.* New York: Norton and Company.

Avneyon, E. (2005). *Dictionary of world mythology.* Tel Aviv: Itiav Publishing House (Hebrew).

Backer, B. A., Hannon, N. R., & Gregg, J. Y. (1994). *To listen, to comfort, to care: Reflection on death and dying.* Albany, NY: Delmar Publishers, Inc.

Baider, L., Cooper, C. L., & Kaplan, D-N. A. (Eds.). (2000). *Cancer and the family.* New York: John Wiley and Sons.

Bard, M. G. (2006). *Myths and facts online: A guide to the Arab-Israel conflict.* Jewish Virtual Library: AICE.

Bergman, Z., & Cohen, E. (1994). *The family—In search of equilibrium.* Tel Aviv: Am Oved Publishers (Hebrew).

Berlioz, H. (1966). *Berlioz's mémoires.* New York: Dover Publications. (Reprint of the 1932 Knopf edition)

Blanchard, C. G., Albrecht, T. L., & Ruckdeschel, J. C. (1997). The crisis of cancer: Psychological impact on family caregiver. *Oncology*, February, 189–194.

Bloom, B. (1964). *Stability and change in human characteristics.* New York: John Wiley & Sons.

Bowlby, J. (1969/1973/1980). *Attachment and loss.* London: Hogarth.

Breznitz, S. (1983). *The denial of stress.* New York: New York University Press.

Bright, R. (2002). *Supportive eclectic music therapy for grief and loss. A practical handbook for professionals.* St. Louis: MMB Music, Inc.

Bruscia, K. E. (1998). *Defining music therapy* (2nd ed.). Gilsum, NH: Barcelona Publishers.

Buckman, R. (1996). Talking to patients about cancer. *British Medical Journal*, 313, September 1996, 699–700.

Burk, J. N. (Ed.). (1939). *Great concert music.* New York: Plenum Press.

Chipp, H. B. (Ed.). (1971). *Theories of modern art: A source book.* Berkeley, CA: University of California Press.

Colman, A. M. (2001). *Oxford dictionary of psychology.* Oxford: Oxford University Press.

Davies, A., & Richards, E. (2003). *Groups in music: Strategies from music therapy.* London: Jessica Kingsley Publishers.

Dickinson, E. (1890). *Favorite poems.* New York: Avenel Books.

Dor, M. (1978). *Maps of time.* London: The Menard Press.

Dorland, W. A. (1982) *Dorland's illustrated medical dictionary* (26th ed.). Toronto/Tokyo: Igaku–Shoin/Sounders International Edition.

Eliram, T. (2002). Eretz Israel songs. In Bartal, I. (Ed.), *The full carriage: A century of Israeli culture* (pp. 236–243). Jerusalem: Magnes Press of the Hebrew University (Hebrew).

Elizur, S., Tyano, H., Munitz, M., & Neumann, M. (Eds.). (1990). *Selected chapters in psychiatry.* Tel Aviv: Papyrus Publishing House (Hebrew).

Erez, T. (1993). Risk factors: The etiological model and psychological educational intervention in early childhood. In Levenson, S. (Ed.), *Psychology in school and in the community* (p. x). Tel Aviv: Hadar (Hebrew).

Faber, S., & Tur-Paz, S. (Directors). (2006). *Burial and mourning. ITIM for a democratic society.* Jerusalem: The Jewish Life Information Center.

Freud, S. (1917). Mourning and melancholia. In *Sigmund Freud: Collected papers* (Vol. 1, pp. 152–173). New York: Basic Books.
Freud, S. (1921). Group psychology and analysis of the ego. In Elizur, S., Tyano, H., & Munitz, M. (Eds.), *Selected chapters in psychiatry,* 1990 (pp. 449–461). Tel Aviv: Papyrus Publishing House (Hebrew).

Freud, S. (1938). Splitting of the ego in the defensive process. In *Sigmund Freud: Collective papers* (Vol. 5, pp. 372–375). New York: Basic Books.

Gal–Pe'er, A. (1978). Let's sing Hebrew: On kindergarten Hebrew songs from the age of linguistic revival. In *Literature of children and adolescents* (Fourth year, no. 3, pp. 3–17). (Hebrew).

Gibran Khalil Gibran (1923). *The prophet.* New York: Knopf.

Gibran Khalil Gibran (1933). *The garden of the prophet.* New York: Knopf.

Gombrich, E. H. (1971). *The story of art.* London: Phaidon Press (Hebrew).

Gradenwitz, P. (1996). *The music of Israel: From the biblical era to modern times.* Portland, OR: Amadeus Press.

Grant, S. (2005). *Standing on his own two feet.* London: Jessica Kingsley Publishers.

Griffiths, P. (1986). *20th-century music.* New York: Thames and Hudson.

Hacohen, E. (1982). *Levin Kipnis and the Hebrew song: Studies in the work of Levin Kipnis.* Tel Aviv: Levinsky College of Education (Hebrew).

Hed, S. (1991). *A guide to opera.* Tel Aviv: Dvir Publishing House (Hebrew).

Hirshberg, J. (1974). *Music and drama in opera.* Jerusalem: Tcherikover and The Institute of Arts at The Hebrew University of Jerusalem (Hebrew).

Hirshberg, J. (1990). *Paul Ben Haim, his life and works.* Jerusalem: Israeli Music Publication.

Hunt, M. (2005). Action research and music therapy: Group music therapy with young refugees in a school community. In *Voices: A world forum of music therapy, 5*(2), July.

Javlensky, A. (1948). *Der blaue reiter.* In *Das kunstwerk II,* 1948. ArtCyclopedia Online, 2006.

Kaplan, H. I., & Sadock, B. J. (1982). *Modern synopsis of Comprehensive Textbook of Psychiatry III.* Baltimore, MD: Williams & Wilkins Company.

Kastenbaum, R. (1974). Childhood: The kingdom where creatures die. *Journal of clinical child psychology,* Summer, 11–14.

Klein, M. (1989). *Narrative of a child analysis.* London: Virago Press. (First published in 1961 by Hogarth Press)

Klingman, A. (1998). *Death and bereavement in the family.* Jerusalem: Henrietta Zold Institute (Hebrew).

Kübler-Ross, E. (1969). *On death and dying.* New York: McMillan Publishing.

Langer, S. K. (1982). *Philosophy in a new key. A study in the symbolism of reason, rite, and art* (3rd ed.). Cambridge, MA: Harvard University Press.

Laplanche, J. & Pontalis, J-B. (1985). *The language of psycho-analysis.* London: The Hogarth Press and The Institute of Psycho-Analysis.

Laurent, S. (2004). The great pictorial movements: Expressionism and futurism. *Bohème Magazin. An online magazine, 1*(11), March.

Lelior, A. (2004). *Till death do us part.* Tel Aviv: Ministry of Defense (Hebrew).

Maguire, P. (1985). Barriers to psychological care of the dying. *British Medical Journal, 291,* 1711–1713.
Manne, S. (1998). Cancer in the marital context: A review of the literature. *Cancer Investigation, 16*(3), 188–202.

Meyer, L. B. (1956). *Emotion and meaning in music.* Chicago and London: The University of Chicago Press.

Milgram, N. (2000). Children in a stress situation. In A. Klingman, A. Raviv, & B. Stein (Eds.), *Children in stress and in emergencies: Characteristic and psychological interventions* (pp. 13–57). Jerusalem: Ministry of Education, Psychological and Counseling Services (Hebrew).

Mintz, R. F. (Translator and editor). (1968). *Modern Hebrew poetry. A bilingual anthology.* Berkeley and Los Angeles: University of California Press.

Minuchin, S. (1974). *Families and family therapy.* Tel Aviv: Reshafim (Hebrew).

Miron, D. (1987). The place of Neomi Shemer in our life. In *If Jerusalem didn't exist* (pp. 175–206). Tel Aviv: Hakibbutz Hameuchad (Hebrew).

Nectoux, J. M. (Ed.). (1984). *Gabriel Fauré: His life through his letters.* London: Marion Boyaes Publishers.

Neumann, M. (Ed.). (1990). In S. Elizur, H. Tyano, M. Munitz, & M. Neumann (Eds.), *Selected chapters in psychiatry.* Tel Aviv: Papyrus Publishing House (Hebrew).

Noy, P. (1999). *Psychoanalysis of art and creativity.* Tel Aviv: Modan Publishing House.

Noy, S. (2000). Models for understanding the reaction of trauma as a help in identifying principles of treating trauma and post-trauma. In A. Klingman, A. Raviv, & B. Stein (Eds.), *Children in stress and in emergencies: Characteristic and psychological interventions* (pp. 57–143). Jerusalem: Ministry of Education, Psychological and Counseling Services (Hebrew).

Parkes, C. M. (1972). *Bereavement—Studies of grief in adult life.* New York: International Universities Press, Inc.

Pavlicevic, M. (2003). *Groups in music—Strategies from music therapy.* London: Jessica Kingsley Publishers.

Peterson, K. C., Prout, M. F., & Schwartz, R. A. (1991). *Post-traumatic stress disorder: A clinician's guide.* In *The Plenum Series in Stress and Coping.* New York: Plenum Press.

Plach, T. (1980). *The creative use of music in group therapy.* Springfield, IL: Charles C. Thomas Publishers.

Ratenaude, A. F. (2000). A different normal: Reaction of children and adolescents to the diagnosis of cancer in a parent. In L. Baider, C. L. Cooper, & D. Kaplan (Eds.), *Cancer and the family* (pp. 239–253). New York: John Wiley and Sons.

Reshef, Y. (2004). *The early Hebrew folksongs. A chapter in the history of modern Hebrew.* Jerusalem: Bialik Institute (Hebrew).

Robertson, S. (2006). *Ornamentation and symbols on Israeli gravestones.* Study Sphere: http://www1.unihamburg.de/RRZ/rrz_info/mitarbeiter/Srobertson.html

Rolvsjord, R. (2005). Collaboration on songwriting with clients with mental health problems. In F. Baker & T. Wigram (Eds.), *Song writing:*

Methods, techniques, and clinical application for music therapy clinicians, educators, and students (pp. 97–116). London: Jessica Kingsley Publishers.

Ron, H. (1993). The Israeli song—In constant search after a musical identity. In Y. Mar-Haim & Y. Stavi (Eds.), *All Gold* (pp. 21–24). Tel Aviv: Sifriat Maariv.

Rosenheim, E. (1990). *A man meets himself—Psychotherapy: Experience and process.* Tel Aviv: Schocken Publishing House (Hebrew).

Rosenheim, E. (2003). Mourning and condolence. In *My heart goes out for you—Psychology encounters Judaism* (pp. 172–249). Tel Aviv: Yediot Acharonot (Hebrew).

Rubin, S. (1990). Death of the future. An outcome study of bereaved parents in Israel. *Omega, 20,* 323–339.

Rubinstein, H. L., Chon-Sherbok, D. C., Edelhei, A. J., & Rubinstein, W. D. (2002). *The Jews in the modern world.* Oxford: Oxford University Press.

Sapoznik, H. (1999). *Klezmer: Jewish music from Old World to our world.* New York: Schirmer Books.

Satir, V. (1989). *Peoplemaking.* Tel Aviv: Sifriat Hapoalim (Hebrew, 15th ed.).

Schneider, M. (2003). *Writing my way through cancer.* London: Jessica Kingsley Publishers.

Sekeles, C. (1990). *Music as a therapeutic agent: The Developmental-Integrative Model in music therapy.* Doctoral dissertation. Jerusalem: The Hebrew University.

Sekeles, C. (1994). The many faces of the drum. *Therapy Through the Arts, The Journal of the Israeli Association of Creative and Expressive Therapies, 1*(3), 7–19.

Sekeles, C. (1995). The voice of the body—Reflection of the soul. *Therapy Through the Arts, The Journal of The Israeli Association of Creative and Expressive Therapies,* 2 (1), 6–16.

Sekeles, C. (1996). *Music: Motion and emotion.* St. Louis: MMB. Since 2005, Gilsum, NH: Barcelona Publishers.

Sekeles, C. (1996/1997). Music and movement in Moroccan healing rituals. In K. Hörmann (Ed.), *Yearbook of cross-cultural medicine and psychotherapy* (pp. 55–63). Berlin: Verlag für Wissenschaft und Bildung.

Sekeles, C. (2000). Shamanic rituals: Origins and meaning. *Therapy Through the Arts, The Journal of The Israeli Association of Creative and Expressive Therapies,* 3 (1), 90–107.

Sekeles, C. (2002). *Musical improvisation as a therapeutic language.* Unpublished presentation for clinical psychologists. Jerusalem: Ministry of Health.

Sekeles, C. (2005a). *Voice and silence.* Unpublished presentation. In A Desert Time: ICET General Conference, April 7–19, 2005, Arad.

Sekeles, C. (2005b). *From passive mutism to creative inner song (a therapeutic process with a chronic schizophrenic patient).* Unpublished presentation. Florence, Italy: Shir Association Conference, September 26, 2005.

Shahar, N. (1999). *The Israeli song—Its birth and development in the years 1920–1950.* In Z. Shavit (Ed.), *Structuring a Hebrew culture in Israel* (pp. 495–533). Doctoral dissertation. Jerusalem: The Hebrew University. (Hebrew)

Siegel, J. P., & Spellman, . (2002). The dyadic splitting scale. *The American Journal of Family Therapy, 30*(2), March–April, 93–100.

Siepmann, J. (1995). *Chopin: The reluctant romantic.* London: Victor Gollancz. Read in: http://en.wikipedia.org/wiki/chopin

Silverman, P. R., & Worden, J. W. (1992). Children's reaction in the early months after the death of a parent. *American Journal of Orthopsychiatry, 62,* 93–104.

Slavson, S. (1952). A textbook on analytic group pschotherapy. New York: International University Press. (1st ed., 1943).

Smilansky, S. (1981). *Children's view of death.* Haifa: Ach (Hebrew).

Sogyal Rinponche (1993). *The Tibetan book of living and dying.* New York: Harper Collins Publishers. (Hebrew translation, 1996, Tel Aviv: Gal Publishing Ltd.)

Spann, C. (2004). *Poet healer. Contemporary poems for health & healing.* Sacramento, CA: Sutter's Lamp.

Stein, D., & Avidan, G. (1992). *The unconscious effort of a parent to preserve the psychopathology of his child.* Bat–Yam: Abarbanel Psychiatric Hospital.

Strunk, O. (1950). *Source readings in music history. From classical antiquity through the romantic era.* New York: Norton & Company.

Tatelbaum, J. (1984). *The courage to grieve.* New York: Harper & Row.

Wiess, C. (2004). Using Israeli songs in music therapy to build inner and interpersonal communication with youths suffering from various disabilities. *Therapy Through the Arts, The Journal of The Israeli Association of Creative and Expressive Therapies, 3*(2), 77–85.

Wigram, T. (2004). *Improvisations. Methods and techniques for music therapy clinicians, educators, and students.* London: Jessica Kingsley Publishers.

Wigram, T. (2005). Song writing methods—Similarities and differences: Developing a working model. In F. Baker & T. Wigram (Eds.), *Song writing: Methods, techniques, and clinical application for music therapy clinicians, educators, and students* (pp. 246–265). London: Jessica Kingsley Publishers.

Wilde, O. (1890). *The critic as an artist. Collected works of Oscar Wilde.* USA: Wordsworth Collection.
Winnicott, D. W. (1971). *Playing and reality.* Harmondsworth, UK: Penguin Books.

World Health Organization. (Ed.). (1996). *The ICD–10 classification of mental and behavioural disorders: Clinical descriptions and diagnostic guidelines* (1st ed., 1992). Geneva: World Health Organization.

Yalom, I. (1985). *The theory and practice of group psychotherapy.* New York: Basic Books.